JOHN WESLEY

WOMEN OF FAITH SERIES

Amy Carmichael
Corrie ten Boom
Florence Nightingale
Gladys Aylward
Hannah Whitall Smith
Isobel Kuhn
Mary Slessor
Joni

MEN OF FAITH SERIES

Borden of Yale
Brother Andrew
C. S. Lewis
Charles Finney
Charles Spurgeon
Eric Liddell
George Muller
Hudson Taylor
Jim Elliot
Jonathan Goforth
John Hyde
John Wesley
Martin Luther
Samuel Morris
Terry Waite
William Carey
William Booth

John and Betty Stam

JOHN WESLEY

"I look upon the world as my parish"

Basil Miller

Introduction by Stephen W. Paine

BETHANY HOUSE PUBLISHERS
MINNEAPOLIS, MINNESOTA 55438

ISBN 0-87123-272-3

Published by Bethany Fellowship, Inc.
6820 Auto Club Rd., Minneapolis, Minnesota 55438

INTRODUCTION

Often when it seems that Satan's empire is firmly entrenched, and when the forces of righteousness seem to be losing morale and carrying on a futile rearguard action, somewhere behind the lines God is quietly preparing and "furnishing thoroughly" a man for His purpose. Then at the proper strategical point, not too soon and not too late, He brings forth His instrument and delivers to the kingdom of darkness a series of blows which rock it upon its base.

Thus it was with Moses who spent forty years in God's desert school while all his people forgot him. So, too, with David and John the Baptist and Paul. And the life of John Wesley, the father of Methodism, is another case in point.

God needed a man like Wesley for a particular time and purpose. Patiently He worked over this frail human instrument, gave him the proper abilities and childhood training and a splendid university background, deflated his complacency and self-sufficiency through the humbling sojourn in America, gave him a hunger and thirst for God's holiness which would not be denied and then brought him forth as a stentorian evangel of full salvation.

Dr. Miller rightly interprets the changing scenes of Wesley's life as the unerring dealings of God with this great man, and he thus gives new meaning to those events which are all too frequently dealt with as simply "so much biographical stuff."

As we read this stirring portrayal of God's dealings with Wesley, we shall do well to remember that our heavenly Father is no respecter of persons and that He can make of even us a vessel unto honor, sanctified and meet for the Master's use, if we are but willing to die completely to self and to become yielded clay in the great Potter's hands.

STEPHEN W. PAINE

Houghton, N. Y.

CONTENTS

Chapter I

THE RECTORY LAD

He came into the world the son of the leanest of the lean English rectories. He went out of the world having enriched it with the vibrancy of his redeemed personality. As a youth he saw his father imprisoned because of debt, yet in his age the world owed him such an obligation of gratitude that time cannot repay it.

Born in a home where the scant necessities of life were luxuries, when he left the world for heavenly scenes of labor, he bequeathed it his possessions — two silver spoons, a silver teapot, a well-worn frock coat and *the Methodist Church.*

This John had run the gauntlet of human experience. From poverty to soul riches he had traveled. From a hand-sculptured childhood he climbed to the position of masterminding the outstanding spiritual revolution of the modern ages. It was all there — a hungry childhood, of which he says, "From ten to fourteen I had little but bread to eat, and not a great plenty of that" — a glorious old age, when in his eighties he thought nothing of "walking six miles to keep a preaching appointment."

In between were the grandest adventures in Christian experience to be found in all the records of soul pilgrimages. Living on a massive scale in the realm of rebuilt personalities, this John had walked the low roads when in Georgia he was a stranger to grace's transforming power, and had climbed to the heights where "the Spirit bears witness with my spirit that I am a son of God."

He was the product of the Epworth rectory, but before his sun should set and his good-night be spoken, he had taken the world as his parish and had dotted its face with heaven-touched churches. At the Charterhouse School the older boys "stole my bread," in the vigor of manhood the mobs stoned him, but at his tomb in the City Road Chapel Cemetery, which his bones have consecrated, men bow in solemn acclaim.

Born the son of Samuel and Susannah, the world took him to her bosom as one of her brightest lights. He met God at Aldersgate, and was thereby created anew. Going out to his world parish, he re-chiseled the channel through which time's stream was to flow. . . .

John's outward life began June 28, 1703, at Epworth where his father was rector. But the real roots of the man are to be found in a long line of resident forces which came down to him from a distinguished ancestry. On both the paternal and maternal side his heritage was marked by the influences of several outstanding ministers.

John wrote to his brother Charles, thirty years after the date of organized Methodism, saying, "So far as I can learn, such a thing has scarce been these thousand years before, as a son, father, grandfather, *atavus*, *tritavus*, preaching the Gospel, nay, the genuine Gospel, in a line." Here he refers to his several grandfathers who were preachers of the true Gospel.

If great men are born of a noble heritage, then assuredly John qualifies for such a position. His father Samuel was a preacher, who though constantly in debt, stood as a towering man in his generation. An Oxford graduate, he found time to write several books, which were to be overshadowed by those of his famous son.

John's grandfather on his father's side of the house was John Wesley, an Oxford man and an exceptional student, who as a Nonconformist strenuously defended his views of the right to become a minister without Episcopal ordination. Back of him stood his father Bartholomew Wesley, a Puritan clergyman in the Established Church on whom Oxford had placed its stamp.

These spiritual and scholarly forces concentrated in the person of John produced the Oxford Methodist, who was to sire that spiritual revival which saved England from a social upheaval matching in ferocity the French Revolution.

Equally impressive are John's forbears on his mother's side of the family. Susannah herself was a noble woman, not only because of her high spiritual endowment, but because of a brilliant and thought-germinating mind. Had the fire of 1709, where John refers to himself as "a brand plucked from the burning," not destroyed her notes and her literary output, those writings would have carved for her a niche in woman's hall of renown.

While yet in her teens she knew Greek, Latin and French and had saturated her mind with theology. She had read the Early Fathers and was wrestling with metaphysical innuendoes while other girls were still playing with dolls. This ability she inherited from her father, Dr. Annesley, a Puritan minister, who has been called "the St. Paul of the Nonconformists."

When a friend inquired how many children Dr. Annesley had, Thomas Manton, who had been baptized one of the family, answered, "I believe it is two dozen or a quarter of a hundred." And Susannah was that quarter-of-a-hundred child. The last, she was the most gifted of the children and the most beautiful as well.

She married Samuel when nineteen and in the next twenty-one years gave birth to nineteen children. They had begun their wedded life on an income of approximately $150 a year. With the rapidly growing family, poverty always stared the curate in the face. Many years later Mr. Wesley wrote to his bishop saying that he had but fifty pounds a year for six or seven years and "one child per annum."

It was into this home that John was welcomed as the fifteenth child, the second son, to be followed by a third son, Charles, as the seventeenth child. One evening while they were checking the family treasury, wife and husband discovered that between them they could muster but six shillings, this in face of the soon-arriving twins.

Asked once while Samuel was lying in prison for debt whether she ever wanted bread, Susannah replied to the Archbishop of York, "My lord, strictly speaking, I never did want bread. But then I had so much care to get it before it was eaten, and to pay for it after, as has often made it very unpleasant to me; and I think to have bread under such terms is next degree of wretchedness to having none at all."

John was his mother's son and it was from her rather than from Samuel that he inherited those traits of character which were to set him apart from ordinary men. Samuel was a faithful shepherd of his Epworth flock, consisting of some two thousand souls, but Susannah possessed the spark of religious genius which was to inflame her son's soul.

At the time of John's birth his brother Samuel was a lad of thirteen and on his way to Westminster School, and the elder Samuel was busy writing his *History of the Old and New Testament, in Verse.* Before his to-be-famous son was three, Father Wesley was thrown into jail for debt, and many were the disturbing factors the Wesleys were to face during those Epworth years.

It was a most orderly household into which John made his entrance. Susannah's mind was the soul of order and system. She might be able to read Greek, nonetheless at home she clocked off family details with the punctuality of a machine. The children were put into a regular manner of living even from birth. When very young so deft was her control that her offspring were taught "to cry very softly."

Said Susannah, "I insist on conquering the will of children betimes, because this is the only strong and rational foundation of a religious education, without which both precept and example will be ineffectual, but when this is thoroughly done then is a child capable of being governed by the reason and piety of its parents, till its own understanding comes to maturity, and the principles of religion have taken root in the mind."

Little John, along with the other toddlers and older children, as soon as he was able to talk on arising and just before retiring said the Lord's Prayer, to which were by degrees added short prayers for his parents, some collects, a short catechism, and such portions of the Scripture as his memory could contain and his mother should direct.

Susannah had assistance in this religious instruction, for the oldest took the youngest that could speak, and the second oldest the next youngest, to whom were read the psalms for the day and a chapter in the New Testament. John along with his brothers and sisters were taught to be quiet at family prayers.

Eating and drinking also came under Susannah's careful oversight, for she limited the children to three regular meals a day with no piecing betimes. Eight o'clock was bedtime for young John and servants were not permitted to sit by his bed until he fell asleep. This was a task he must perform by himself.

When John was five, as was Susannah's custom with each child, he learned the alphabet. For this his mother set aside but one day, and on the following day began spelling and reading from the Bible with the book of Genesis as the starter. As he progressed, stress was laid on good reading and correct writing. To these mental exercises in time were added the multiplication tables, elementary mathematics, grammar and history.

It was during these early years that John laid the foundation for facility in grammer from which was to flow later grammars for the study of English, French, Latin, Greek and Hebrew, all of which he composed.

It was when John was six that the memorable fire occurred at Epworth which burned the rectory. On the night of February 7, 1709, the family was awakened by flames which were eating through the house. All the children with their elders rushed outside as Susannah supposed, but on checking she discovered one was missing. Soon framed in a window on the second floor stood little John.

There being no ladder handy, a peasant suggested that someone climb on his shoulders and thus rescue the child, which was done. Just as John was landed safely on the ground the roof collapsed. In later years he refers to himself as a "brand plucked from the burning." This experience he felt, when age had seasoned his mentality and time had spoken to his soul, was the hand of Providence in preparing him for giving birth to Methodism.

The children were early made to distinguish between Sunday and other days, and when praying, even though they could not yet speak they were taught to ask a blessing by the use of signs. Susannah stored John's mind with Scripture, taught him diligently the meaning of right-doing and shielded his childhood from association with other rowdy youth.

It was her custom to set aside a certain time weekly for the religious instruction of each child, and John's hour came on Thursdays when she carefully interviewed the young "Jackie."

Susannah, assisted by the Reverend, was the sole teacher of the girls, and the boys as well until they were later sent to school in London. Never was there a child who did his teacher more credit than John.

Between eight and nine he had smallpox, which he endured in a manly manner, enough so to cause his mother to write to Samuel then in London, "Jack has borne his disease bravely, like a man, and indeed like a Christian, without complaint."

While the rector was attending Convocation in London, Susannah decided that there should be a church in her house; so she began conducting divine services each Sunday at the rectory. During these meetings she would read good books and sermons to her children. The neighbors hearing about it decided they wanted to attend.

Rector Samuel in London hearing of this oddity wrote his wife dissuading her from the practice. The mother of Methodism replied in defending her actions:

"It is plain, in fact, that this one thing has brought more people to church than ever anything did in so short a time. We used not to have above twenty or twenty-five at evening service, whereas we have now between two and three hundred, which are more than ever came before. . .

"Besides the constant attendance on the public worship of God, our meeting has wonderfully conciliated the minds of this people toward us . . . they are much reformed in their behavior on the Lord's day, and those who used to be playing in the streets now come to hear a good sermon. . .

"I need not tell you the consequences if you determine to put an end to our meeting. . ."

Nor were the meetings discontinued, for the soul of Susannah was aflame with holy zeal not only to do good to her own family but to those of the rector's charge. John partook of this sterner moral quality of his mother, rather than of the complacency of his father. Even as a child he was scaled after the model of his mother.

"Sweetheart," said Father Samuel to his wife, "I profess I think our boy Jack would not attend to the most pressing necessities of nature unless he could give a reason for it."

It was this quality which marked Wesley's path through the eighteenth century. The methodical, argumentative child was the Methodist Wesley in embryo.

Childhood days could not last forever, and however great Susannah's ability as a school marm, she did not profess to be a wizard at the art of training her boys.

Nor did the Oxford graduate Samuel feel content that his sons should be less trained than he. So when Samuel, Jr., was thirteen he was sent to Westminster in London to advance his studies.

John, doubtless a brighter lad than Samuel, started his educational career at the famous Charterhouse School, London, when ten and a half. This beneficence was through the friendly services of the Duke of Buckingham.

Samuel, a wandering cleric, was often in London and left the management of his parish to Susannah with the assistance of a curate. Doubtless Susannah and the growing John looked upon the jaunts as a waste of the minister's time. There was one trip, however, he made which was not all lost. And that was the London *safari* during which he obtained the scholarship for John. Concerning this he writes:

"I've a younger son at home whom the Duke of Buckingham has this week written down for his going into the Charterhouse as soon as he's of age: so that my time has not been all lost in London."

That younger son was John. Though the letter was written when John was eight, still he was assured of an open road toward a qualifying education for whatever task he should undertake in his mature years.

When Methodism's future sire entered Charterhouse he was in no wise handicapped by a lack of routine or formal training. For the private education he had received from Mother Susannah not only taught him learning from books but drilled into his system, both mental and spiritual, the principles of plain living and high thinking. At this time he was "a diligent and successful scholar and a patient and forgiving boy, who had at home been inured not indeed to oppression but to the hard living and scanty fare."

John was admitted as a charity scholar on the Sutton Foundation, along with forty-three other boys who were unable to pay their way. He received his meals in the dining hall and being small for his age, the older boys robbed his platter of the tastier morsels.

"From ten to fourteen," John later writes, "I had little but bread to eat and not great plenty of that. I believe this was so far from hurting me that it laid the foundation of lasting health."

Samuel fearing for the boy's health admonished his son to "run around the green three times each morning," which advice the lad followed to the letter, making this turn of about a mile each day.

While the youthful Wesley was busy polishing his mind he became lax in keeping his religious diligence up to par. Rather than abetting his religious growth his stay at Charterhouse had the reverse effect.

This caused him to say, "Outward restraints being removed, I was much more negligent than before, even of outward duties, and almost continually guilty of outward sins, which I knew to be such, though they were not scandalous in the eye of the world. However, I still read the Scriptures, and said my prayers morning and evening. And what I now hoped to be saved by was — (1) not being so bad as other people; (2) having still a kindness for religion; and (3) reading the Bible, going to church and saying my prayers."

Tyerman in commenting on John's stay at Charterhouse doubtless overdraws the picture of Wesley's character derelictions when he says, "Terrible is the danger when a child leaves a pious home for a public school.

John Wesley entered the Charterhouse a saint, and left it a sinner."

It was during this time that spooky noises were being heard at the Epworth rectory. Often while at prayers there would be rattlings in the building, knocks and loud jars, which caused the family to go so far as to name the rambunctious spirit "Old Jeffery."

John was a diligent student at this time, for Samuel, Jr., writes to his father saying, "Jack is a brave boy, learning Hebrew as fast as he can." Charterhouse, however, was but the springboard into the broader world of education and training for John. Finishing his course there in 1719 he was soon on his way to Oxford, where his life was to be chiseled by the hammer of divine providence.

Chapter II

THE OXFORD DON

Wesley entered Christ Church, Oxford, on June 24, 1720, receiving a scholarship of approximately $200 a year, or £40. It was this along with a few scant gifts from the Epworth homefolk that made his university days possible. Oxford did little to improve John's spiritual life.

In reality the university had struck one of the low levels of its scholastic and religious history, and had little to offer the student save a boarding place, a room in which to study and lectures to attend. Degrees were given for residence on the basis that the university was inhabited by students and residence implied the habit of study.

Gibbon entering Oxford forty years later said of his stay, "They proved the fourteen months the most idle and unprofitable of my whole life . . . The fellows . . . from the toil of reading, or thinking, or writing, they had absolved their conscience. . ."

Little is known of John's undergraduate life, save that due to his lack of money he lived almost as a recluse. A contemporary describes him as "a very sensible, active collegian, baffling every man by the subtleties of his logic, and laughing at them for being so easily routed; a young fellow of the finest classical tastes, of the most liberal and many sentiments, gay and sprightly with a turn for wit and humor."

Here he was to remain until after his ordination as deacon in 1725. Wesley makes little reference to his studies, but he gives us to understand that his religious life was little better than during his Charterhouse days.

"I still said my prayers," he remarks, "both in public and private; and read, with the Scriptures, several other books of religion, especially comments on the New Testament. Yet I had not all this while so much as a notion of inward holiness; nay, went on habitually and for the most part very contentedly in some or other known sin; though with some intermission and short struggles, especially before and after Holy Communion which I was obligated to receive twice a year."

When John went to Oxford his health was far from being robust. He frequently suffered from nosebleeds, and in a letter to his mother in 1723 he told her how he had almost choked from the bleeding while walking in the country. He began reading Dr. Cheyne's *Book of Health and Long Life*, which "condemns eating anything salt or high-seasoned, as also pork, fish, stall-fed cattle; and recommends for drink two pints of water and one of wine in twenty-four hours, with eight ounces of animal and twelve of vegetable food in the same time. The book is chiefly directed to studious and sedentary persons." John as a dutiful son writes to his mother of this new food routine.

To this book the mature Wesley owed a debt of gratitude which he tries to repay, forty-six years after reading, in these words, "How marvelous are the ways of God. How He kept me from a child . . . When I grew up in consequence of reading Dr. Cheyne I chose to eat sparingly and drink water. This was another great means of continuing my health till I was about seven and twenty. I then began spitting blood . . . A warm climate (Georgia) cured this. I was afterwards brought to the brink of death by a fever; but it left me healthier than before. Eleven years after I was in the third stage of a consumption; in three months it passed. Since that I have known neither pain nor sickness, and am healthier than I was forty years ago."

At the time of his sickness his mother wrote him, saying, "Be not discouraged; do your duty, keep close to your studies, and hope for better days . . . we shall pick up a few crumbs for you before the end of the year."

In this last sentence she referred to her Jackie's constant financial embarrassment. He had just taken his bachelor's degree at Oxford and this occasioned added expense which had exceeded the small budgetary limits his scholarship placed upon him.

When John was twenty-two, the year after taking his degree, he came to a turning point in his career. Living under Susannah's constant oversight and training until he was ten, he found implanted in his heart a bearing toward the ministry. Nor could it be thought singular that such was the case, since his heritage had brought down to him stories of those time-defying curates who had marked his ancestry. He could not have been Samuel's son and not inclined toward the pulpit, much less Susannah's pupil.

This bent toward the ministry as a life occupation came to the fore in 1725. Though he was outwardly a churchman, still the flame of divine fire flickered low in his life during his educational career. For more than twelve years he had been away from home, living in an atmosphere of culture and training. This had dulled the keen edge of his religious sentiments.

He had become a gay collegian, a favorite in any society, a wit, whose repute for scholarship was high, but whose religious life was indifferent. Late one evening he met the college porter, a deeply pious man, with whom the don began to speak. The poorly clad porter was urged to go home for a coat, the evening being cold. In return the porter thanked God for the one coat he had on, as well as for water — his only drink during the day. When John asked him what else there was to be thankful for, said the porter, "I will thank Him I have the dry stones to lie upon."

Being urged by John to continue, the servant said, "I thank Him that He has given me my life and being, a heart to love Him, and a desire to serve Him."

Returning to his room that evening John began to feel there were emotional depths to salvation he had not plumbed. He was a stranger to such sentiments. He wrote to his parents about this urge to enter the life of a cleric. His father replied that he should not enter the priestly office "just to have a piece of bread."

Susannah knowing the spiritual weakness of her son became more personal in her response. She had trained him to see the beauty in religion, the glory of Christian service, but she realized also that having left her bed and board long years since, he had departed from much of his deeply pious attitude toward Christian service and experience.

"I heartily wish you would now enter upon a serious examination of yourself," she admonished, "that you may know whether you have a reasonable hope of salvation by Jesus Christ. If you have, the satisfaction of knowing, it will abundantly reward your pains; if you have not, you will find a more reasonable occasion for tears than can be met with in a tragedy."

There were deep springs of spiritual overflowing down in Susannah's heart which kept bubbling to the surface in the form of advice to her son. She had taught him aright while directing his early education, and now beyond the pale of her immediate influence, she wanted young John to be certain of his relationship to Christ. In reality it was her own experience of redemption through Christ that mothered the Methodist revival.

Samuel in thinking it over decided to add to the warnings he had previously sent his son, so he wrote again, saying, "The principal spring and motive . . . must certainly be the glory of God and the service of the Church in the edification of our neighbor. And woe to him who with any meaner leading view attempts so sacred a work."

John's heart was warmed toward such sentiments, for recently he had been reading Thomas a Kempis' *Imitation of Christ*, and Taylor's *Holy Living and Dying*, as he was later to read Law's *Christian Perfection*. These books awakened his conscience, and began to toll a bell in his mind, the burst of whose melody had but faintly sounded since leaving home.

"The providence of God," writes Wesley, "directing me to Kempis' *Christian Pattern*, I began to see that true religion was seated in the heart, and that God's law extended to all our thoughts as well as words and actions . . . I set apart two hours a day for religious retirement. I communicated every week. I watched against all sin, whether in word or deed. I began to aim at and pray for inward holiness. So that now, 'doing so much and living so good a life,' I doubted not but I was a good Christian."

Again he speaks of this book's influence upon his life, affirming, "I resolved to dedicate all my life to God . . ."

Reading Taylor's works gave birth to another important phase of Wesley's life, that is, the writing of his Journals, which in confessional literature stand with Augustine's *City of God*, or any heart-revealing memoirs and journals of the ages. These he wrote partially in cipher, some in abbreviated longhand, and partly in shorthand. They were penned for his own reading and not for the public eye, though it was the public which finally made them famous.

The first diary begins with the following rules and resolutions, written in John's exquisite hand:

A General Rule in All Actions of Life

Whenever you are to do an action, consider how God did or would do the like, and do you imitate His example.

General Rules for Employing Time

1. Begin and end every day with God; sleep not immoderately.
2. Be diligent in your calling.
3. Employ all spare hours in religion, as able.
4. All holidays (holy-days).
5. Avoid drunkards and busybodies.
6. Avoid curiosity, and all useless employments and knowledge.
7. Examine yourself every night.
8. Never on any account pass a day without setting aside at least an hour for devotion.
9. Avoid all manner of passion.

Friday, March 26. I found a great many unclean thoughts arise in prayer (or devotions), and discovered these temptations to it:

a. Too much addicting myself to light behavior at all times.

b. Listening too much to idle talk, or reading vain plays or books.
c. Idleness, and lastly want of devotion . . . from which I perceive it is necessary:
    a. To labor for grave and modest carriage;
    b. To avoid vain and light company; and
    c. To entertain awful apprehensions of the presence of God.
    d. To avoid idleness, freedom with women and high-seasoned meats;
    e. To resist the very beginnings of lust, not by arguing with, but by thinking no more of it or by immediately going into company; lastly
    f. To use frequent and fervent prayer.

General Rules as to Intention

1. In every act reflect on the end.
2. Begin every action in the name of the Father, the Son and the Holy Ghost.
3. Begin every important work with prayer.
4. Do not leave off a duty because you are tempted to do it.

At its heart this is the source of the Methodist revival, and though the hand is John's, the voice is Susannah's. It was this methodical manner of dealing with his own soul, the springs of his emotions, the curbing of his passions, the exalting of God through prayer that in the end was to produce Aldersgate. John had not yet arrived at complete religious satisfaction through a personal experience of salvation, but he was definitely on his way.

Thus his life standard takes the form of critical self-analysis, rule and resolution. Sometimes at Oxford and later when serving as his father's curate at Wroote, he holds a private session with his own soul, and on a Saturday night reads his resolutions and performs an inquest upon his motives and emotions. He makes complete confession of these sins and shortcomings at the bar of his own conscience.

"Never," says Curnock in his introduction to the Standard Edition of Wesley's Journal, "does he have mercy upon himself. Not once does he excuse himself or enter a single plea in extenuation . . . Nothing daunts him. Saturday night finds him in the depths, but on Sunday morning he is bravely beginning again. Defeat and failure always seem to stimulate Wesley to new effort."

John might have been constitutionally lazy, but he forced himself to be out of bed by four o'clock each morning, and seldom did he arise later than five. By the use of his diary he lashed himself to a careful accounting of his time, so that he would waste not a moment.

Once he made up his mind to seek ordination, he became diligent in his religious duties. It was in the midsummer of this year while preparing for his ordination that he won his first convert. He had gone out with a close friend to attend the funeral of a young woman, and the conversation was steered toward religion. John wrote to his mother that he persuaded him "to let me have the pleasure of making him a whole Christian . . ."

John's message shot to its target and the young man was converted. Eighteen months later he died, and it was John's blessed privilege to preach the funeral sermon of this his first convert.

Wesley's ordination as a deacon took place on Sunday, October 19, 1725, at Oxford in Christ Church Cathedral at the hands of Bishop John Potter, and as priest on September 28, 1728. Once ordained he was not slow in beginning his active ministry, and his first sermon was preached shortly at South Leigh. Forty-six years later he had the privilege of preaching at the same place and one of the original congregation was present.

Long afterwards he wrote of his ineffective early preaching, saying, "Preaching was defective and fruitless, for from 1725 to 1729 I neither laid the foundation of repentance nor of preaching the Gospel, taking it for granted that all to whom I preached were believers, and that many of them needed no repentance. From 1729 to 1734, laying a deeper foundation of repentance, I saw a little fruit. But it was only little — and no wonder; for I did not preach faith in the blood of the covenant."

The following spring after his ordination he was elected a Fellow of Lincoln College, which brought glad news to the family in the Wroote rectory, to which they had temporarily moved, and though Rector Samuel had but twenty-five dollars to keep his family until the harvest, still he was in high spirits.

From March 16, 1726, when he was so elected, Wesley always referred to himself as a Fellow of Lincoln College, placing this designation on the title page of his books. This was an appointment of which he was rightfully proud.

John settled down to his academic duties with characteristic sobriety and vigor. He wrote to his mother, "Leisure and I have parted company," to which one of his biographers adds, "and they never met again." Mondays and Tuesdays were devoted to Greek and Latin, Wednesdays to logic and ethics, Thursdays to Hebrew and Arabic, Fridays to metaphysics and natural philosophy, Saturdays to oratory and poetry, Sundays to divinity.

He was appointed Greek lecturer and moderator of the classes, which required him to preside over the class debates. "I could not avoid," he said, "acquiring hereby some degree of expertness in arguing, and especially in discovering and pointing out well-covered fallacies. I have since found abundant reason to praise God for giving me this honest art."

The following year he obtained his master of arts degree, acquiring considerable reputation because of his disputation for the diploma.

He unhappily learned that his money did not increase in proportion to his scholastic standing, for it was necessary for him to save ten dollars a year by allowing his hair to grow long, thus warding off the expense of a wig, much to the amazement and despair of Susannah.

His father was now sixty-five and in ill health, and was in need of a curate to assist him with the double parishes at Epworth and Wroote; so he asked the loan of John from the university. At the same time the Fellow had a position offered him in a school with a good income, but he felt that it was God's will for him to answer his father's call, and so he spent two and a half years as curate at Wroote. He returned at intervals to Oxford when it was deemed necessary for him to be present.

During one of these journeys he barely escaped being drowned, and once he traveled several miles to walk with a "serious man," who told him, "The Bible knows nothing about solitary religion." His brief stay at Wroote was all the parochial experience John was ever to have.

Conditions were such at the university that he was ordered back to take up the duties of his fellowship, arriving on November 22, 1729. Here he continued until his embarkment to Georgia in 1735.

Having served his apprenticeship, God was ready for John's soul to be molded into such a methodical symmetry that he was to be called "the methodist."

It was during these years that Wesley read William Law's *Christian Perfection,* from which later was to spring the germs of his own doctrine of sanctification. Law, however, inclined toward pietism, and Wesley at first enamored of Law's writings, soon forsook him.

Chapter III

THE HOLY CLUB

While John was serving as his father's curate at Wroote, great things were happening at Oxford, which as a strange providence were to give birth to Methodism. Wesley's soul was longing for the highway that led to religious freedom. He was striving outwardly to conform his life to spiritual standards, while the inner glow making this possible failed to spark into flame.

John's youngest brother Charles had come to Christ Church in 1726, and has been described as being a young man with "more genius than grace." When John tried to bring his brother's life more under the influences of religion, Charles was quick to object to "becoming a saint all at once."

During John's curacy something happened at Oxford which turned Charles' mind toward religion, and began to slant his character forces toward higher goals. Writing to his brother at Wroote, he said:

"There is no one person I would so willingly have to be the instrument of good to me as you. It is owing . . . to somebody's prayers (my mother's most likely) that I am come to think as I do; for I cannot tell myself how or why I awoke out of my lethargy, only that it was not long after you went away."

Charles turned seriously to his studies, marking his life with an attitude of one who faced terrific soul problems that could be solved only by a studious attempt at learning and holiness. He began to attend the Sacraments weekly and to induce others to join him in this search for righteousness. He and his companions adopted rules for the governing of their lives, directing their religious activities, alloting their time carefully for study and churchly duties. In this time-charting they gave little attention or space allocation to sleep or food, and as much as possible to religion.

It was a small group that circled around Charles, but their weekly trip to Oxford cathedral caught the attention of an undergraduate who said, "Here is a new set of Methodists sprung up."

Charles says the word *Methodist* "was bestowed upon himself and his friends because of their strict conformity to the method of study prescribed by the university." However the name was first used as, and in its connotation it came to bear, an opprobrious designation, and later when John referred to it, he did so with a consciousness that it was used in a derogatory manner.

In an early sermon John speaks of his associates as "the people in derision called Methodists." In his English Dictionary he defines a Methodist as "one that lives according to the *method* laid down in the Bible."

On October 21, 1729, Dr. Morley, the Rector of Lincoln, informed Wesley that as a junior fellow he must attend to his duties in person, and sent him an invitation to return to Oxford. On returning to the university John found the little group of Methodists in action, and at once became their leader.

His age as well as his scholarship made it inevitable that he should assume this position. Various names were applied to these methodical religionists as fellow students viewed them. Some spoke of them as Sacramentarians, Bible Moths, Bible Bigots; two names, however, rapidly gained the ascendancy — Methodists and the Holy Club.

John was nicknamed "curator of the Holy Club," or sometimes "the father of the Holy Club." Samuel now in his declining years on hearing of this said, "If this be so . . . I am the grandfather of it; and I need not say that I had rather any of my sons should be so dignified and distinguished than to have the title of 'His Holiness.' "

Oxford began by laughing at the idea of these "Bible Moths," who made it a rule daily to read the Bible and to attend Communion weekly, but this ridicule was shortly to burn into alarm. Early in 1731 a meeting of some senior members of one of the colleges was held for the purpose of discussing what methods could be used to check this enthusiasm. Gradually the news was spread that these censors were to "blow up the Godly Club," which of course they were unable to do.

The first work of the Holy Club was Bible study. While other items were on the agenda, the searching of the Scripture was the paramount one.

"From the very beginning," said Wesley, "from the time that four young men united together, each of them was *homo unius libri*, a man of one book . . . They had one and only one rule of judgment . . . They were continually reproached for this very thing, some terming them in derision Bible Bigots, others, Bible Moths, feeding, they said, upon the Bible as moths do on cloth . . . And indeed . . . it is their constant endeavor to think and speak as the oracles of God."

This was to be the fundamental issue in the growth of Methodism, and wherever you find John during the long decades of his career, he was still a Bible Moth.

So great was this love of the Bible that in his later life he wrote his *Notes on the New Testament,* which in its day was a classic and created a favorable impression outside Methodist ranks.

The members of the club at first met Sunday evenings, and this in time became a twice-weekly session when they gathered for Bible study and discussion. At length these meetings became nightly, from six to nine o'clock. Those famous sessions were begun by beseeching God's benedictions upon their lives. After this prayer season they opened their Greek Testament for a period of searching the Scripture in the original language. This was followed by a brief study of the classics. The evening was climaxed by a detailed review of the day, an outlining of tomorrow's tasks and, finally, a frugal supper.

Along with the weekly celebration of the Lord's Supper, they also set aside two days each week for fasting and prayer, and laid out a set of rules by which each member was to try himself before the bar of conscience:

1. Have I embraced every probable opportunity of doing good and of preventing . . . evil?
2. Have I thought anything too dear to part with to serve my neighbor?
3. Have I spent an hour at least every day in speaking to someone?
4. Have I in speaking to a stranger explained what religion is not . . . and what it is, the recovery of the image of God?
5. Have I persuaded all I could to attend public prayers, sermons, sacraments?
6. Have I after every visit asked him who went with me: Did I say anything wrong?
7. Have I when anyone asked my advice directed and exhorted him with all my power?

8. Have I rejoiced with and for my neighbor?
9. Has goodwill been . . . the spring of all my actions
   toward others?

This chart of self-guidance is a worthy ideal for
attaining and diligently did John try to align his outward life and inner soul with its regulations. He lived
with such severity that often one wonders whether he
did not do himself a grave injustice. Later when charity
was added to the list of activities the Club engaged in,
John lived upon £28 of the £30 he received during the
year, and gave away the money thus saved. However
much he might make, even up to $600 a year (or £150),
he still lived upon the original $140, and gave the rest
away.

It was this diligence in keeping his outward life con-
formed to his spiritual idea that was the source of his
power with others. As the Holy Club leader John realized that great was his responsibility not only for rules
but for building those regulations into living experiences.

William Morgan, one of the members, visited a man
who was condemned for the murder of his wife. While
in the castle jail he also conversed with debt prisoners
and became convinced that good might be done among
them. He passed his ideas on to the other members of
the Holy Club. The result was that the Wesley brothers
went with Morgan to the jail on August 24, 1730 — a
visit which resulted in their taking a special interest in
prisoners. Morgan also took upon himself the burden
of visiting the sick, which in turn became a mark of the
Holy Club's social activities.

When John met a poor girl in destitute circumstances,
he asked, "You seem half starved; have you nothing to
cover you but that thin linen gown?" The girl replied,
"Sir, this is all I have." John's hands went to his pocket

for money, but came out empty. Going to his room he
studied the pictures on the walls, which seemed to
accuse him of unfaithfulness in the matter of charity.

From this came the Holy Club's practice of giving
all they could to alleviate the human sufferings of
others. This principle remained with Wesley to the end
of his life, and wherever he went, charity was a leading
tenet of his practical living.

At first there were only four members of the Holy
Club; the following year two or three other members
were added. From time to time the membership fluctu-
ated more or less according to the activities of the
Wesleys and other members in drawing friends to their
organization. Only three of the various members are
today entitled to a position on memory's shelves of
fame. The rest have long since been pigeonholed and
remain only in dull and heavy tomes of erudition.

Charles, the founder, we remember as John's brother,
which alone was not enough to entitle him to fame; for
it must also be remembered that John had an older
brother, Samuel, Jr., an Oxonian whom time has easily
forgotten. Charles became the singer of the Methodist
revival as John was to be its organizer. The third member was George Whitefield, the outstanding evangelist
and preacher of his generation. Whitefield joined the
Holy Club through a kindness of Charles in loaning him
a book to read, which burned through the outward shell
of his religious life and set aflame the passions of his
soul. No man since Paul has been more entitled to
fame as a preacher than Whitefield.

George was the son of a tavern keeper, whose Christian mother asked him to lead the singing one day for

a women's meeting. From this kind request George's feet were turned toward the Cross. Arriving at Oxford when eighteen, time ripened his friendship with Charles and at length he became a new creature in Christ.

"I found and felt in myself that I was delivered," he says, "from the burden that had so heavily oppressed me . . . The Daystar arose in my heart. I know the place; it may perhaps be superstitious, but whenever I go to Oxford I cannot help running to the spot where Jesus Christ first revealed Himself to me and gave me a new birth."

This was 1735, the year he cast his lot with the Holy Club.

During these Holy Club years John remained in residence at Lincoln College until 1735. He engaged in various activities, such as holding a curacy in 1730 for a while near Oxford. His constant companion was Charles with whom he had begun to converse in Latin, a custom which they kept up throughout their lives.

Together the brothers walked in 1731 to Epworth, a distance of seventy-five miles. Twice during that and the next year John visited London where he called on William Law, to whom he owed a debt of intellectual as well as spiritual gratitude, joining also while in London the Society for Promoting Christian Knowledge.

During 1733 John wrote two sermons which are of enticing doctrinal import and mark a milestone in his theological thinking. The first of these was on the need of the influences of the Holy Spirit to convert the soul. This is the doctrine which Peter Bohler was to impress on John's mind in 1738.

"The circumcision of the heart," writes the Holy Club father, "is that habitual disposition of soul, which in the sacred writings is termed holiness; and which directly implies the being cleansed from sin, from all filthiness both of flesh and spirit; and by consequence, the being endued with those virtues which were also in Christ Jesus; the being so renewed in the image of our mind, as to be perfect as our Father in heaven is perfect."

This in plainest terms was Wesley's doctrine of Christian perfection, germs of which he had dug from the writings of his friend William Law. "This sermon," he says in 1765, "contained all that I now teach concerning salvation from all sin, and loving God with an undivided heart." Further on in the sermon he says, "He alone (the Spirit) can quicken those who are dead unto God and breathe into them the breath of Christian life . . . Those who are thus by faith born of God have also strong consolation through hope. This is the next thing which the circumcision of the heart implies: even the testimony of their own spirit, with the Spirit which witnesses in their hearts, that they are the children of God."

Here in this sermon, "The Circumcision of the Heart," Wesley lays the foundation of the two doctrines upon which the superstructure of his dogmatic position is to be erected: Christian perfection and the witness of the Spirit. The latter doctrine is John Wesley's one original contribution to the body of Christian belief.

The second sermon is on the Holy Spirit who is justly given the rightful position of import in the Christian's life. "From Him flow all grace and virtue, by which the stains of guilt are cleansed, and we are renewed in all holy dispositions, and again bear the image of our Creator," he says.

In the same year John issued his first printed production, "A Collection of Forms of Prayer for Every Day in the Week," the first of some two hundred publications to be brewed in the seething crucible of his fertile mind.

John was called that year to visit his sick father at Epworth, and as had been the case when he and Charles were previously at the home rectory, the membership of the Holy Club dwindled from twenty-seven to five. It seemed the fate of the Club was bound up with the close oversight of John and Charles. When John later sailed for Georgia the membership stood at thirteen.

Wherever else he might go, and however demanding the calls made upon him elsewhere, John's true love and the loadstone that drew him was Oxford. For here he must have realized God was helping him to find himself and was carving a path for the weary feet of his soul to tread that in the end was to lead to that transforming experience of Aldersgate, around which his life was to pivot.

It was in 1734 that this test came to a head. John's father, Samuel, was sick, and the end seemed to be leaning upon the corner of the Epworth rectory. Word was sent out for one of the boys to come hastily and take his place, else the roof should pass from over Susannah's graying head. And, of course, Sam, now ensconced in a lucrative post as headmaster of Tiverton Grammar School, could not think of leaving his position.

So they turned to John with the plea that he should come and bury his life as Samuel before him had done in this lean $1,000-a-year parish. Here Samuel had spent nearly forty years caring for the souls of his people . . . here nineteen children of his had flowered . . . here Susannah and he had grown old together.

And it was more than he could bear to see the living slip out of the Wesley family.

Samuel, Jr., wrote John implying that since he was "despised" at Oxford he could do more good at Epworth, to which John at once replied: "1. A Christian will be despised anywhere. 2. No one is a Christian until he is despised. 3. His being despised will not hinder his doing good, but much further it, by making him a better Christian. 4. Another can supply my place better at Epworth than at Oxford, and the good done here is of a far more diffusive nature, inasmuch as it is a more extensive benefit to sweeten the fountain than to do the same to particular streams."

John had felt that his life was placed rightly in God's will in Oxford; no pull of a parental nature could lure him from the university, and in her halls he stayed until God was ready for him to move.

About this time he began a practice which was to follow him through life, that of reading on horseback. During the year he rode horseback more than a thousand miles, making excursions to various parts of the country, preaching on Sundays and during the weekdays devoting himself to the care of souls wherever he might find them.

When Father Samuel was seventy-two he was confined to his bed and his sons were sent for. On his deathbed he said to John, "The inward witness, son, the inward witness — this is the proof, the strongest proof of Christianity." Peacefully on April 24, 1735, as the sun was showering the west with gold, Samuel's soul was conveyed to the heavenly regions, while on the next day his body was laid to rest in the Epworth cemetery. Over the grave was placed a modest tombstone which later was to be more famous as John's pulpit than as Samuel's tomb-marker. For from it when Epworth was closed to Samuel's son, John preached his sermon.

Returning to Oxford John and Charles devoted themselves to reviving the decaying fortunes of the Holy Club and to bringing out an English edition of Kempis' *Christian Pattern.*

Shortly the fate of the Club was to hang in the balance when the Wesleys sailed for America. For awhile Whitefield held the group together until in 1738 he followed his friends over the sea, to add luster to his own name. And one by one members departed for other spheres of service, until the Club was no more.

It had served its purpose by being the cradle of Methodism. Some looked upon its first four members as being the charter members of the Methodist Church. Nevertheless it threw around John an atmosphere of piety where his own faith could germinate. Through three of its sons of genius, John, Charles and George, gradually the spark of the Holy Club blazed at Oxford, showered forth across England, leaped to America and the great revival was on.

Philosophically the basic doctrines of justification by faith and the witness of the Spirit had already been written into John's soul, yet they were not living experiential facts. Dogmatically he knew the doctrine but he had not yet experienced it as a soul-transforming power. How to make this transmutation he was to learn from a humble Moravian preacher.

Forty years after this time when John and Charles left Oxford, John wrote of their going forth:

"Two young men without a name, without friends, without either power or fortune, set out from college with principles totally different from those of the common people, to oppose all the world . . . and to combat popular prejudices of every kind. Their first principle directly attacked all wickedness; and their second all the bigotry in the world.

"Thus they attempted a reformation, not of opinions . . . but of men's tempers and lives; of vice of every kind; of everything contrary to justice, mercy, or truth. And for this it was that they carried their lives in their hands; and that both great, vulgar and the small looked upon them as mad dogs and treated them as such."

The trail that John and Charles blazed on this mission of reformation is worthy of our following. First John must bungle in Georgia, return home as a complete failure and then meet God at Aldersgate.

CHAPTER IV

GOD AND JOHN IN GEORGIA

A golden chain of divine purpose binds the life of Wesley into a solid unity, and wherever you prick beneath the skin of John's soul you will find the links existing. John was God's man for a decisive hour, but he was an unmade man, who needed the tutoring of the Holy Spirit to prepare him for the Almighty's plan. Oxford, the Holy Club and now Georgia were God's crucibles to mold John for his great adventure.

Back of the Georgia move was God, and even though Wesley bungled, out of it came deep-seated truths which were to flower into experience. Had there been no Georgia soul-culture when John found he could not make a success of his spiritual life without the Spirit's personal aid, there might have been no Aldersgate.

John's pre-Georgia religion was one of rules — rules unsparked by the divine *afflatus*. It took the humiliating experience of failure beyond the sea to teach John this needed yet costly lesson. Inadvertently it was Samuel who seeded the germ out of which John's over-the-sea life was to come.

Poor old Samuel was deep in Job during the tremendous times that marked his end. While not struggling with duns and debts he was belaboring himself with Job's adversities and ill-starred acts. It proved beyond the strength of the infirm man; so when he completed his manuscript on Job, there was no energy to see the ponderous thing through the press. This he left to John.

Off the press, John tucked the six hundred-page *Dissertations in Librum Jobi* in his saddle bags and hied himself to London where he personally presented it to Queen Caroline, who with permission served as patron for dedication and inscription. Caroline, busy with her maids when John arrived, tossed the book on a window seat, while John on bended knees looked on in suspense. Arising, he left the scene, somewhat downcast that the last labors of his father should be so lightly cast aside.

However out of the London *Librum Jobi* venture came the meeting with General Oglethorpe, who had founded the Georgia colony in 1732. Seeing the need of a missionary in the new land he returned to England in search of a suitable chaplain. Through Dr. Burton of Corpus Christi College, he was introduced to Wesley, and promptly offered him the position.

John took it under advisement, for his own soul had recently been stirred by doubts and longings which he hoped might be resolved and fulfilled in the new colony. He spoke to his brother Charles, and wrote to Susannah. In the Wesley line there had always been missionary interests, for John's grandfather Wesley was stirred with a burning desire to go to Surinam or Maryland. And Samuel himself had devised a mission for India, China and Abyssinia. Even a year before his death he had lamented the fact that he had not a sufficient lease on time to undertake missionary adventures in Oglethorpe's new colony.

On writing to Susannah, she replied in those memorable words, "Had I twenty sons, I should rejoice that they were all so employed, though I should never see them more." This tipped the scales of John's wavering mind and he decided to go.

On October 10, 1735, four days before embarking for America, he gave in a letter his reasons for the venture. "My chief motive," he wrote, "is the hope of saving my own soul. I hope to learn the true sense of the gospel of Christ by preaching it to the heathen. . .

"A right faith will, I trust, by the mercy of God, open the way for a right practice. . .

"I then hope to know what it is to love my neighbor as myself . . . I have been a grievous sinner from my youth up . . . but I am assured if I once be converted myself, God will then employ me both to strengthen my Brethren and to preach His name to the Gentiles.

"I cannot hope to attain the same degree of holiness here, which I may there. . ."

Herein the sire of Methodism clearly outlines his own spiritual condition. He recognizes the high standard of inner holiness God would have him attain, but seems unable to reach it while in England. He hopes, and how vainly we shall see, to find the source of Christian rest and satisfaction by an outward venture which he looks upon as a doleful sacrifice.

Taking Charles as the general's secretary and Ingham of the Holy Club, John embarked on the *Simmonds*, a not-too-large vessel, for the new colony. God had timed his going so that he was to travel with twenty-six Moravians, who were to play a fascinating role in leading John to Aldersgate. There were also some eighty English colonists on board. Though they left Gravesend in October it was December before they got away from England, and weeks were spent on the Isle of Wight waiting for a man-of-war to convoy them.

This gave the Holy Club members plenty of time to outline their day's activities as carefully as they had done in Oxford. This was not to be a mere pleasure trip to John and Charles, for they looked upon themselves as pilgrims to the heavenly land, and whether at the university or on the ship, on land or sea, they strictly practiced their rules of right living.

Four to five each morning was devoted to private prayer, followed by two hours of general Bible study, wherein they compared the Bible with the writings of the Fathers. Breakfast and public prayers took up two hours and from nine to twelve John studied German, his brother wrote sermons and their companion taught the emigrants' children. Throughout the rest of the day these soul-weary voyagers allocated time to good deeds and religious practices as diligently as though they faced an impending peal from Gabriel's trumpet. At evening they joined with the Moravians in a service of devotion.

As God sent a whale for Jonah, so He whirled across the path of John's boat a raging storm. Had the boat been heavier, or the storm not blown up with the fury of doom riding in its wake, Wesley's soul travail might have been told far otherwise than we today read of it. But the storm came and the boat being light rocked on the blood-curdling waves of the deep. John was distraught . . . the passengers despaired of their lives . . . the crew pictured the horrors of Davy Jones's locker.

While the storm was raging, John looked at the Moravians, whom previously he had thought of as heavy-minded and dull-witted folk, and they were calmly singing a hymn. The wilder the waves became, the calmer the Germans sang. The storm passed as all of God's storms do when their missions are fulfilled. But the storm in Wesley's turbulent soul could not be quieted by the soothing efficacy of a still sea.

Going to the Germans he asked them, "Were you not afraid?"

"I thank God, no," came the answer from one whose soul had been anchored to the Rock of Christ.

Then John wondered if the women and children were afraid, for he thought the strong man might have found a source of quietude in his physical vigor. So John asked, "But were not your women and children afraid?"

Answered the man, "No, our women and children are not afraid to die."

John had been previously thinking about his soul's welfare, and when a storm arose on November 23, he entered in his diary, "Sun. 23. At night I was awakened by the tossing of the ship . . . and plainly showed I was unfit, for I was unwilling, to die."

But when he had gone through that sail-ripping, ship-soaking, skin-drenching storm and had come out alive, he was certain those Moravians had an experience to which he was a total stranger. This discovery was a startling one and at the close of that day he entered in his Journal, "This was the most glorious day which I have hitherto seen."

Its glory nestled in the fact that John had sighted the Light. It was a distant Light, but for the first time he knew of its true existence. It was this Light which at Aldersgate was to become a personal experience.

The rest of the journey was uneventful, and when the ship docked on February 6, 1736, Wesley was not long in knowing that there was something wrong with his own Christian holiness. The following day he met the Moravian pastor, Spangenberg, whom John at once sought out for a religious conference.

Spangenberg's first question rocked John back on his mental heels when he asked, "My brother, I must first ask you one or two questions. Have you the witness within yourself? Does the Spirit of God bear witness with your spirit that you are a child of God?" Those questions were new to Wesley, even though he had implied the possibility of this witness in a previous sermon; yet the basis of his implication was theoretical and not experimental.

Again the Moravian asked, "Do you know Jesus Christ?" This was closer to John's thinking, and so he replied, "I know He is the Saviour of the world." "True" came the pastor's rejoinder, "but do you know He has saved you?"

This was a leading question, the answer to which John did not know; so he hedged by saying, "I hope He has died to save me," to be countered by Spangenberg's "Do you know yourself?" John finally managed to mumble, "I . . . do."

This left a blank in the Moravian's mind and set the mental machinery of John's cranium whirling for two years trying to produce a true basis in his own life for the doctrines he preached. He could not get away from Spangenberg's question, and it was only when his heart "was strangely warmed" at Aldersgate that he was satisfied with his own "I do" answer. When he made the entry in his Journal, he added, "I fear they were vain words." But after Aldersgate he not once again questioned his personal salvation. It was this assurance of salvation which gave wings to his words and produced the revival that we know as Methodism.

Nor was John a slow or negligent cleric once he set about his duties. He preached his first sermon on the thirteenth chapter of I Corinthians. The courthouse serving as church was crowded, and John so warmed to his subject that his parishioners listened — and listening, began to tremble. Their cleric was not afraid to declare the whole truth and sharply he began cutting away the foundation from under their sinful lives. A stir struck Savannah, then a town of some forty houses built on the bluff above the river.

So powerful were the effects of his first work that a dance which was to be given ten days later was canceled, for the church was full of prayers and the ballroom empty. He then turned on costly clothing and jewelry with such ferocity that the ladies finally decided to attend the Reverend's services clad only in plain linen or woolen garments.

John not only was a denunciatory pulpiteer, but he looked about for practical methods by which he could do good. He at once established schools, teaching one himself and turning another over to Delamotte who had made the journey from England with the company. When Delamotte's boys got to wrangling among themselves because some had shoes and others none, John exchanged with the pedagogue and came to school barefooted himself. The boys stared, but Wesley kept them at their work, and before the end of the week he had cured the lads of their vanity.

John was very pleased, and so he wrote to Charles, "I have hitherto no opposition at all; all is smooth, and fair and promising," later to add the sentiment, "Savannah never was so dear to me."

But that was before he began bungling and especially before he had hefted himself into the career of his first love. John being a High Churchman could not get it out of his system, and he began to let his Anglicanism come to the fore, even to crowd justice and good sense to the rear. He went so far as to refuse the Lord's Supper to all who had not been Episcopally baptized. Nor would he bury those who had not received the Church of England's seal of acceptance by the rite of baptism.

Years later when the folly of his ways had caught up with him, he said, "Can anyone carry High Church zeal higher than this? And how well have I been since beaten with mine own staff." These antics in the New World could produce but one end and that was ostracism from the group. Charles and his companion had already gotten themselves into a tangle which involved Oglethorpe as having been guilty of moral indelicacy with two women of the colony.

This only added to John's fire, for when John visited one of the women, she asked him to sit down, though he noticed she kept her hands behind her back.

As John was seated she whipped a pistol out, and said, "Sir, you have wronged me, and I will shoot you through the head this moment. . ."

John leaped at her, grasped the gun from her hand, only to confront a pair of sharp scissors in the other. After a tussel with the woman, John faced the constable and Dr. Hawkins, the woman's husband, who asked, "What did the scoundrel do in my house?"

When the unhappy affair was smoothed over by the general, John had fairly well disqualified himself for spiritual leadership in the colony. Charles, with the general at Fredericia, a hundred miles south of Savannah, had become so involved that he was shortly returned to England with dispatches from the governor, and that was the last Georgia saw of him.

John's remaining sentence in Georgia (as he began to look upon his stay there) was not all lost. For he began reading *Pandectae Canonum Conciliorum,* which turned his attention to the Scripture as the source of religious authority. He also heard a Presbyterian minister at Darien actually offer an *extempore* prayer. This shocked and astonished John at first, only in the end to help him realize that such praying in public freed the soul from the mere confines of a set ritualistic approach to God.

"Religion is love," he said to a friend at this time, "and peace and joy in the Holy Ghost . . . so it is the cheerfulest thing in the world . . . utterly inconsistent with moroseness, sourness and with whatever is not according to the gentleness of Christ Jesus."

This, however, he had not discovered in the springs of his own soul, merely quoting these words from the memory of having read them somewhere. Or if he did experience the true meaning of religion as joy and peace in the Spirit, he was soon to go through a tragical relationship with Sophia Hopkey that was to take all the joy out of his religion.

John met the attractive young lady, niece of the Savannah magistrate, and with the quickness of lightning, cupid's arrow found a mark in the cleric's heart. Wooing her, he soon won her promise of marriage. Then

on consulting Moravian friends, the priest changed his
mind. Mind-changing, so it is asserted, being the privilege of the fairer sex alone, Miss Sophia took exception
to John's pre-empting her prerogative. There was something about the Georgia lassie which made a lasting
imprint upon John's mind, for even in old age he wrote
of his disappointment, "I was pierced through as with
a sword."

Sophia soon married another man, and swore out a
warrant for John's arrest. The trial uncovered a lot
of already forgotten experiences which other members
of the colony had suffered at John's High Church hands,
which in nowise added to the minister's reputation.

However, all of John's time in Georgia was not lost,
for he published his "Collection of Psalms and Hymns"
for general congregational use. In a preface to a reprint
it is suggested that this is the first collection of hymns
in the English language, "so that in this provision for
the improvement of public worship . . . Wesley led
the way." Among the songs were some of his father's
which had been rescued from the Epworth fire, as well
as translations Wesley made from the German.

When the storm of that trial broke there was only
one thing for John to do, and that he did at once —
left for England. He was a somber cleric, his soul shot
through with doubts when on December 2, 1737, he
left the colony for Carolina on his way home. He had
failed, and he knew it as no other person. The high
religious standards he had set to attain in the Holy Club
had eluded his spiritual grasp. He could not get to
them.

The entry in his Journal under date of Tuesday,
January 24, 1738, is tragical:

"I went to America to convert the Indians; but O! who shall convert me? Who, what is he that shall deliver me from this evil heart of unbelief? I have a fair summer religion. I can talk well; nay, and believe myself while no danger is near; but let death look me in the face, and my spirit is troubled. Nor can I say, 'To die is gain' . . . I show my faith by my works by staking my all upon it . . . O who will deliver me from this fear of death?"

When he landed in England on the first of February, his soul once more wallowed in the Slough of Despond, of which his Journal tells the turbulent story thus:

"This then have I learned in the ends of the earth, that I 'am fallen short of the glory of God'; that my whole heart is 'altogether corrupt and abominable' . . . that my own works, my own suffering, my own righteousness, are so far from reconciling me to an offended God . . . I want that faith which enables everyone that hath it to cry out, 'I live not . . . but Christ liveth in me' . . . I want that faith . . . when 'the Spirit itself beareth witness with his spirit that he is a child of God.'"

It took his Georgia's errors in judgment, his love entanglement which resulted in a court trial, to produce this self-abasement. God had brought John safely by the hand from the high pinnacle when he hoped to work his way into the kingdom, to where now he felt that only through faith in Christ's atoning merit could he live above the storm that would sweep his soul in his terrible tomorrows.

Looking back upon that hour from the vantage point of many years of Christian service, to his first statement, "I, who went to America to convert others, was never myself converted," he adds, "I am not sure of this."

Where John had achieved his least, America had done her best in helping the hand of Providence to shape his career, around the bend of which was to be Aldersgate.

Chapter V

THE HEART STRANGELY WARMED

John before his Georgia mistakes was not a prepared subject for God's soul-dealings, but once having walked the fiery path that led to soul debasement, he was in a condition where God's prophetic voices could be heard. Up until that time John was the Oxford don, the teacher in any group, and as such was discontent to act as learner. Having discovered that as teacher he was as the blind leading the spiritually blind, John was willing to throw himself at the feet of any who possessed the true source of Christian knowledge.

In this condition he was ready to become a spiritual learner, and God was not long in crossing his path with the man who was to serve as his teacher. But before this path-crossing of learner and teacher, there was yet another element which was to enter into the don's training.

George Whitefield, won to the Master through Charles's kindness, had early found the true source of divine power in his life. Finding it, he shone as a brilliant evangelistic light. While John and Charles were failing in America and entangling their lives in petty quarrels and religious embarrassments, George had set to preaching. And when he arose to speak it was as though a breeze from heaven had fanned across the audiences. Groups began to talk and when it was announced the eloquent Oxford evangel was to bring a message, churches were crowded to the doors. The hungry people had never heard the like. Hearing, they went to their homes, only to return and hear more.

George spoke on weekdays, often thirty times a week and usually three or four times a Sunday, and weeping hearers followed him to the streets and to his abode to get a word with him. His message was "the doctrine of the new birth and justification by faith in Jesus Christ (which) made its way like lightning into the hearers' consciences," as Whitefield affirms.

John on hearing of Whitefield's successes persuaded him to come to America with his messages on faith, clear-cut on heaven and hell. "What if thou art the man, Mr. Whitefield?" wrote John from Georgia. "Do you ask me what you shall have? Food to eat, and raiment to put on, a house to lay your head in . . . and a crown of glory that fadeth not away."

Whitefield read the message and decided to join his fellow Holy Club member, only to find that their ships passed in the Atlantic. When John arrived in London he was thrown into contact with some Moravians recently in the work with Count Zinzendorf. Among these was Peter Bohler, trained at Jena and sent out as a missionary by Zinzendorf. Not being able to speak English very well, John decided to assist Peter and his friends to find lodging. This opened up a comradeship which was to have much to do in remaking the path John's soul was to follow.

"I traveled with two brothers, John and Charles Wesley," Bohler wrote to the Count, "from London to Oxford. The elder, John, is a good-natured man; he knew he did not properly believe on the Saviour, and was willing to be taught . . . Our mode of believing in the Saviour is so easy to Englishmen that they cannot

reconcile themselves to it . . . They justify themselves
. . . and try to prove their faith by their works. . ."

While walking together John told the Moravian about
his beliefs, and Peter said, "My brother, my brother,
that philosophy of yours must be purged away." John
was willing to listen to his teacher and was anxious to
find the purging process.

Charles undertook to teach English to Bohler and
while engaged in this endeavor, he fell sick, word being
sent to his brother that he was about to die. Bohler took
advantage of the low physical condition to better
Charles's spiritual life.

"Do you hope to be saved?" asked the Moravian.
When Charles answered "Yes," Peter asked, "For what
reason do you hope it?" Came the answer, "Because I
have used my best endeavors to serve God."

Bohler's answer was merely a shake of his head.
Charles was disconsolate at that shake, for all the foun-
dations of his hope of salvation were thereby expunged.
John rushing to Charles's bedside found the Moravian
present and at once began speaking to him.

"I found my brother at Oxford . . . and with him
Peter Bohler," John enters in his Journal under date
of March 4, "by whom I was on Sunday, the fifth, clearly
convinced of unbelief, of the want of faith whereby
alone we are saved."

This turbulency of soul caused John to despair of
ever preaching again, and he told Bohler that he would
"leave off preaching. How can you preach to others,
who have not faith in yourself?" Bohler urged him to
continue his gospel work, to which John retorted, "But
what can I preach?"

"Preach faith until you have it; and then because you have it, you will preach faith," came the Moravian's response.

John was not long in starting on this adventure, for he says, "Accordingly, Monday 6, I began preaching this new doctrine, though my soul started back from the work. The first person to whom I offered salvation by faith alone was a prisoner under sentence of death."

The condemned man arose from prayer and exclaimed, "I am now ready to die. I know Christ has taken away my sins, and there is no condemnation for me."

John was now willing to go all the way on this new salvation path. He was ready to cast over his forms and rituals where he felt they constrained his spirit in worship. On the following Sunday he took a leap into the light which was to mark an important advance in the history of his work. He tells about this thus:

"Being in Mr. Fox's society my heart was so full that I could not confine myself to the forms of prayer which we were accustomed to use there. Neither do I propose to be confined to them any more, but to pray . . . with form or without as I find suitable to a particular occasion."

This was the birth of the religious freedom which was to mark his followers. The ritualist in him was already destroyed, and the manacles had been torn from his hands of devotion. "Soon the fetters would be broken which bound his feet, and he would be running in the evangelical way." The following Sunday, which was Easter, he preached in the college chapel of Lincoln, using extempore prayer, and he closed the day with the entry in his Journal, "I see the promise, but it is far off."

Week by week John continued his preaching as Sundays rolled around, and meantime his searching went on with diligence. Seeing Bohler again he was urged to find the Pearl of Great Price, which advice Wesley had determined to take. Peter, relying on testimony to clinch his dogmatics, took with him some Christian friends and visited John. Each one gave clear testimony as to what Christ had done for them by changing their lives and transmuting Peter's theories into living, dynamic realities in their souls.

John was thunderstruck, for it seemed too good to be true that here were people in the flesh who possessed what he was seeking, and this convinced him that his search was in the right direction.

"I was now thoroughly convinced," he said, "and by the grace of God, I resolve to seek it unto the end: (1) By renouncing all dependence . . . upon my own works of righteousness, on which I have grounded my hope of salvation . . . from my youth up. (2) By adding to the constant use of all the other means of grace continual prayer for this very thing, justifying, saving faith, a full reliance on the blood of Christ shed for me; a trust in Him as my Saviour, as my sole justification, sanctification and redemption."

This was to be no trip to the halfway house up this rocky road to salvation John was taking. He was determined to stop only when he had scaled the peaks and sat watching the sunrise burst over the hills of God, and felt the glow of redemption as a personal possession within his soul.

Charles caught the sunrise first, after reading Luther's "Commentary on Galatians," praying, conversing with spiritually minded people. It was on Whitsunday, 1738, while he was at the home of a poor woman, a recent convert. Said the woman to the man sick in body and soul: "In the name of Jesus of Nazareth, arise and believe, and thou shalt be healed of all thy infirmities."

A friend read the words, "Blessed is the man whose transgression is forgiven, whose sin is covered." Charles's eyes fell on the verse, "He hath put a new song in my mouth . . ." as the hallelujah chorus swung into living action, and God's redemptive work was accomplished in his soul.

On this Charles's believing and receiving day, John attended the Church of St. Mary-le-Stand, grieving still that his redemption had not taken place. Returning from service, he wrote to a friend, "Let no one deceive us by vain words, as if we had already attained unto this faith. By its fruits we shall know. Do we already feel peace with God and joy in the Holy Ghost? . . . Does the Spirit bear witness? . . . Alas with mine he does not . . . Let us be emptied of ourselves and then fill us with all peace and joy in believing."

He was on a soul search which should cease only when he had found this glorious peace. His spiritual quest went on by the hour until Wednesday, May 24, arrived. Let him tell the story:

"Wed. May 24 — I think it was about five this morning that I opened my Testament on these words, 'There are given unto us exceeding great and precious promises, even that ye should be partakers of the divine nature.'

"Just as I went out, I opened it again on those words, 'Thou art not far from the kingdom.'

"In the afternoon I was asked to go to St. Paul's. The Anthem was, 'Out of the deep have I called unto Thee, O Lord . . . O Israel, trust in the Lord; for with the Lord there is mercy. . .' "

During that memorable soul-shaping day everything seemed to point John to one thing — redemption as a soon-wrought work in his life. When evening came down Aldersgate Street not far from St. Paul's, John was unwillingly dragged to a meeting.

"In the evening," he says, "I went very unwillingly to a society in Aldersgate Street, where one was reading Luther's preface to the Epistle to the Romans. About a quarter before nine, while he was describing the change which God works in the heart through faith in Christ, I felt my heart strangely warmed. . ."

The change had been wrought, the divine work accomplished. He had arrived at the peak's top and there was the sunrise of glory in his soul.

"I felt I did trust in Christ," he goes on to relate, "Christ alone, for salvation; and an assurance was given me that He had taken away my sins, even mine, and saved me from the law of sin and death."

The glory had dawned and John was on his way down the divinely appointed path that should to a world parish lead ere his religious sun set. Emptying himself of self, God had come in. John the bungler now became John, the gospel workman, the mallet of whose soul was to strike the carving chisel of his personality with such sure blows that the statue he sculptured remains as a divinely wrought achievement.

So great was the glory, so marvelous was the change, so grand was the experience that John could not rest until he told it to another. The brazier's house where

Charles was staying being not far distant, John went there with the glad news, which to his soul had become the most wonderful story in the world. Walking into Charles's room he said, "I believe. . ."

That was enough to set the joy bells ringing in Charles's heart, and together the brothers lifted a song. Charles tells the story of this meeting when he says:

"Towards ten my brother was brought in triumph by a troop of our friends, and declared, 'I believe.' We sang a hymn with great joy and parted with prayer."

And that song we may sing today, as it has rung through the ages, a song of triumph and glory.

> Where shall my wondering soul begin:
>   How shall I to heaven aspire?
> A slave redeemed from death and sin,
>   A brand plucked from eternal fire.
> How shall I equal triumphs raise,
> Or sing my great Deliverer's praise?

This was the hymn Charles had begun on the Tuesday following his own conversion, and, with the many hundreds more he was to pen, furnished the music for the spiritual revolution he and John were to sire.

The biographers have debated long and loud as to what really happened at Aldersgate. Some affirm, and these the older, that John there dropped all ritualistic attachment to the Church of England and at that moment Methodism was born.

"Newman renounced justification by faith," affirms Riggs, "and clung to apostolic succession; therefore he went to Rome. Wesley embraced justification by faith, and renounced apostolic succession; therefore his people are a separate people from the Church of England."

Cadman avers, "The priest is merged in the prophet." Lunn would have us believe that "it was not his Aldersgate Street conversion, but precisely those habits which he had formed during that Oxford period of his life . . . which made Wesley 'the most useful saint in the British Empire.' " Canon Overton feels that "if John Wesley was not a good Christian in Georgia, God help the millions who profess to call themselves Christians."

What happened at Aldersgate? It is best to let John's own testimony stand as to the change which his heart-warming experience brought about. Before May 24, 1738, he felt he was not a Christian. After that date, he knew he was, and the Spirit bore witness with his spirit that he was a child of God. The trustworthiness of Wesley's testimony must stand or fall with the trust-worthiness of our consciousness. If the human mind is not conscious of its own awareness as the spotlight of certainty is flashed upon it, then truth is utterly without foundation and hence impossible.

Judged by the products of Wesley's life, Aldersgate stands by far as the brightest spot in his life, or in the life of anyone of his century. Before Aldersgate he was a bungler; after Aldersgate he was a lion in God's kingdom who knew no defeat.

Returning home the night of his Aldersgate transfor-mation, he wrote in his Journal, "I was much buffeted with temptations; but cried out and they fled away . . . And herein I found the difference between this and my former state chiefly consisted. I was striving, yea, fight-ing with all my might under the law as well as under grace. But then I was sometimes, if not often, con-quered; now, I was always conqueror." Fitchett speaks of this entry, "Here was struggle; but here too was victory."

John had received the witness that he was the son of God, and this assurance gave him spiritual boldness. Henceforth he was ready to tackle the job of converting the world by the truth of the message he had experienced. Later he wrote to his brother Samuel, "I believe every Christian, who has not yet received it, should pray for the witness of God's Spirit that he is a child of God. This witness, I believe, is necessary to my salvation."

Wesley has been termed an organizer rather than a theologian, but he did, however, make one distinct contribution to theological science, and that is his doctrine of the witness of the Spirit. The Moravians taught the doctrine, but it remained for John to systematize the dogma.

John was not content to remain idle, once he had planted his feet on the solid rock of Christian assurance. On June 11, eighteen days after his spiritual transformation, he preached before the University of Oxford his famous sermon on "By grace are ye saved through faith." This message sounded the keynote of his lifelong ministry. He knew no other doctrine save this one, and wherever we find Wesley in this post-Aldersgate term of service, this is the message he heralds.

This doctrine of salvation by faith in Jesus to which the Spirit bears witness became the rallying cry of the new movement which he was soon to bring into existence. Before entering his new work, that of being a preacher of experimental salvation, John wished to visit Herrnhut, the colony which Zinzendorf headed and where Moravian activities centered.

His Journal entry for June 7 reads, "I determined . . . to retire a short time into Germany . . . And I hoped the conversing with those holy men who were themselves living witnesses of the full power of faith, and yet able to bear with those that are weak would be a means . . . of so establishing my soul, that I might go on from faith to faith. . ."

From June until September of the year 1738 he spent traveling and visiting Zinzendorf, where he obtained a close-up view of the Moravian work as well as an intimate glimpse into their lives. It is told how Zinzendorf set the thirty-five-year-old convert at digging in his garden, and when the Englishman was bursting with perspiration, the Moravian hied him off to visit another German count. John asked for time to wash his hands and change linen.

Zinzendorf said, "You must be simple, my brother," and left it at that. John's impression from this visit seems not to have borne out the picture he had formed of the Moravians at a distance.

Back home again from foreign wanderings, he set about preaching the gospel with dire earnestness. Wherever an occasion presented itself Wesley was there with his new doctrine of the full assurance of salvation. He found time to preach at the Newgate prison, where he "offered them free salvation," as he expresses it.

At once cudgels were taken up by the ministers against Wesley's doctrine of assurance. Sermons were preached and printed against "those who of late asserted that they who are not assured of their salvation by a revelation from the Holy Ghost are in a state of damnation." Such sermons were certainly heading toward a general refutation of Wesley's work. John, however, was prepared to pay such a price for his religious freedom.

He had already made a beginning of a group which should in the end be the foundation for the Methodist Church. Early in May, 1738, Peter Bohler had advised him to establish a society which should be modeled upon the existing Moravian societies of London. While this was a Church of England society, and by no means were such societies rare things, still it was more closely allied to Moravianism than Anglicanism. When he returned from Herrnhut the membership of the society stood at thirty-two.

Wesley was now in possession of the doctrine of the coming revival. His soul was attuned to the heavenly chorus. Zeal was bursting within and with the foundational society, he was ready for all comers.

During the remaining months of 1738 Wesley's work was composed mostly of acting as religious adviser and confessor. He preached wherever occasion presented, but his doctrines had become so adverse to the ordinary preaching of the day that most ministers closed their churches to his ministry. In all of London there were only three or four churches open to him by the end of that year.

This exclusion is often spoken of as a sign of the Church's decay, for it could not bear with the religious enthusiasm of such a stirring man. This but hardened the steel of John's character, for he knew the doctrine he proclaimed to be declared in the Bible and rooted in his experience. Firmly he preached on, and, as the days passed, a growing consciousness possessed him that his message should be heard more and more by the Fetter Lane Society he had formed at the suggestion of Bohler.

The group held weekly meetings for prayer and discussion. On New Year's Eve, 1738-39, seven of the Oxford Methodists and sixty other people conducted a watch night service and love feast, the results of which were to usher Wesley into a new field of service.

"About three in the morning," says Wesley, describing the service, "as we were continuing instant in prayer, the power of God came mightily upon us, insomuch that many cried out for exceeding joy, and many fell to the ground. As soon as we were recovered a little from that awe and amazement at the presence of His majesty we broke out with one voice, 'We praise Thee, O God, we acknowledge Thee to be the Lord!'"

Whitefield pronounced this to be "the happiest New Year's Day he had ever seen." Three days later the seven ministers, members of the Anglican Church, met again, of which Whitefield writes, "What we were in doubt about after prayer we determined by lot and everything was carried on with great love, meekness and devotion. We continued in fasting and prayer till three o'clock, and then parted with the conviction that God was to do great things among us."

It was the prayer of this Fetter Lane Society that inaugurated Wesley's next move, of which George, and not John, was to be the prime leader. Indeed God was to do great things with the group.

CHAPTER VI

THE WORLD HIS PARISH

When the churches closed their doors to the Oxford preachers, God was opening another gate into which they were to step. It was from this new adventure the revival was to begin. The low state of spiritual life marking church and ministry was used of the Lord to turn Wesley's attention to other fields of Christian endeavor to promote kingdom enterprises. The turning came about on this order.

When Whitefield was twenty-one he was England's most popular pulpit orator. His soul was aflame with the Holy Club message, salvation by faith, and the newness of the doctrine along with the speaker's absolute control over his audiences opened the hearts of the people, as well as their pulpits, to him. John in Georgia felt the need of his preaching friend, and so he wrote George asking him to come to the colony with his fiery messages. Their boats crossed as we have elsewhere indicated.

Whitefield remained in Georgia six months and then returned to London for the purpose of collecting money for an orphanage. Leaving as England's most popular preacher, he expected to be so received again. But he discovered to his amazement that he as well as John had been excluded from the London pulpits. This was difficult for him to understand; so he decided to make a preaching tour to Bristol, where he had previously been very popular.

The Bishop of London told Whitefield that his preaching was tinctured with enthusiasm, as indeed the preaching of the new movement was to be, and by the end of January all churches were closed to him. Arriving at Bristol, the attitude of the London clergy George found had preceded him. He was informed by the chancellor of the diocese that he could not preach in Bristol churches without his license.

"Why did you not require a license from the clergyman that preached last Thursday?" asked Whitefield, to which the chancellor replied, "That is nothing to you."

From church to church the evangelist went requesting a preaching appointment, only in the end to find all Bristol pulpits closed to him. George, a preaching soul, could not have his message stopped by the mere refusal of a stated pulpit. He would make his own pulpit he declared. And that declaration was the beginning of the Wesleyan revival.

Four miles from Bristol was Kingswood where lived a class of men who had never seen inside a church nor heard the voice of a preacher. The colliers of Kingswood were England's worst specimens of humanity. They made up an ecclesiastical no-man's land. On Saturday, February 17, George spoke to two hundred colliers on the Kingswood Common. He defied church rules and fashions by preaching in the open air.

"I thought," he affirms, "it might be doing the service of my Creator, who had a mountain for his pulpit and the heavens for a sounding board; and who, when His Gospel was refused by the Jews, sent His servants into the highways and hedges."

His first audience was small, but the mighty power of the man stirred those colliers' souls and they called for more. When George lifted his voice the fifth time, on the Common before him was an audience of ten thousand. He had found a new pulpit from which no churchly authority could exclude him and an audience which no church could have assembled.

From victory to victory he went until a bowling green in Bristol was offered and here he spoke to eight and ten thousand. The near-by districts called for his open-air preaching, and in some instances he spoke to twenty thousand people. His heart rolled high with enthusiasm, and he decided to defy the London bishop with his new method of preaching.

He faced a dilemma. What would he do with the crowds he had gathered in Bristol and Kingswood? He could not let them be as shepherdless sheep. He decided to call for Wesley. But John with his little circle of London friends was hesitant about taking the step. He did not feel that the outside of a church was so proper a preaching station as the inside. So he referred the case to the Fetter Lane Society. And they, of course, decided it Moravian fashion by opening the Bible at random and taking the significance of the first verse to catch the eye.

John had little luck in his selections. Days earlier he had found this passage by this type of conning the mind of God, "And devout men carried Stephen out to burial and made great lamentation for him." The Fetter Lane verse was, "And Ahaz slept with his fathers, and they buried him in the city, even in Jerusalem." As choice after choice was made the decision seemed more befogged than before.

Wesley decided to go, even though from Bible guidance the trip seemed to lead to his grave. Arriving in

Bristol on March 31, it was difficult for him to take the outdoor step, for in his heart he was still bound by the confines of Anglicanism. Standing by Whitefield as he preached on Sunday, Wesley looked out at the sea of faces before the orator. His heart was moved, for he felt here indeed was an audience to whom God would have him deliver his message.

The next day, April 2, at four in the afternoon John stood on a little eminence outside the city and spoke to three thousand listeners from the text, "The Spirit of the Lord is upon me, because he hath anointed me to preach the gospel to the poor. He hath sent me to heal the broken-hearted; to preach deliverance to the captives, and recovery of sight to the blind; to set at liberty them that are bruised, to proclaim the acceptable year of the Lord."

That was a memorable text and a memorable occasion. In reality it formed the beginning of Wesley's new work. Thinking upon field preaching he brought himself to feel that the Sermon on the Mount "was one pretty remarkable precedent." John had tasted the joy of "field preaching," as it was termed, and he wanted to go back for more of its soul enticement. Here was a crowd of people to whom his message came as a bursting light from heaven, and he would not deny them this glimpse of Christ.

At Bristol, Butler, famous for his *Analogy of Religion,* a scholarly answer to deism, was the bishop. Hearing of Wesley's outdoor work, he decided to challenge the wayward don of Oxford to a controversy. The scholarly bishop, who had devoted much attention to a philosophical sword-bearing against intellectual opponents, did not know how to proceed with this man whose audiences were made up of thousands who had never heard of his *Analogy*.

Butler said, "Mr. Wesley, I deal plainly with you. I once thought you and Mr. Whitefield well-meaning men, but I cannot think so now . . . Sir, the pretending to extraordinary revelations and gifts of the Holy Ghost is a horrid thing — a very horrid thing."

At length the argument went on, Butler thrusting his sword and Wesley countering, until the heated bishop blurted out, "Well, sir, since you ask my advice, I will give it you very freely. You have no business here; you are not commissioned to preach in this diocese. Therefore I advise you to go hence."

Wesley knew the glory of his message and said, "My business on earth is to do what good I can. Wherever, therefore, I think I can do the most good, there I must stay . . . At present I think I can do most good here; therefore here I stay . . . Your lordship knows, being ordained a priest, by the commission I then received, I am a priest of the Church Universal . . . I do not therefore conceive that in preaching here I . . . break any human law. When I am convinced I do, then it will be time to ask, 'Shall I obey God or man?' "

God, always with Wesley, was the last court of appeals. He felt a growing conviction that here was his field of service, and here he determined to remain until God moved him. It took more than a bishop's saying, "Away with you . . ." to change the mind of this man once God had made it up for him.

His one defence henceforth was this, "I obey God rather than man." However great Episcopal censure might be, John cared not for its lash could he only be certain God was saying, "This is the way; walk ye in it."

When brother Samuel heard about this open-air preaching, he too was quite shocked, for he never seemed to catch the meaning of his brother's life or message. John's reply is famous:

"God in Scripture commands me according to my power to instruct the ignorant, reform the wicked, confirm the virtuous. Man forbids me to do this in another's parish; that is, in effect, to do it at all, seeing I have now no parish of my own, nor probably ever shall. Whom then shall I hear: God or man? . . .

"I look upon the world as my parish. Thus far, I mean, that in whatever part of it I am, I judge it meet, right and my bounden duty to declare unto all that are willing to hear the glad tidings of salvation."

This is Wesley's Magna Charta. From thenceforth on he was forever done with bishops when their indictments ran contrary to God's will for his life. And though even to the end he remained a member of the Church of England, still from that hour on he owed no allegiance to it other than to love the organization which had given him ordination. During his lifetime the hours of Methodist services were arranged so as not to conflict with those of the Established Church.

"Wherever there is any Church service," he wrote three years before his death, "I do not approve of any appointment at the same hour, because I love the Church of England, and would assist, not oppose it, all I can."

The Wesleyan meetings in the fields were often scenes of physical excitations, screamings and other unusual occurrences which added to the charge of fanatical excitement. Scenes like the following taken from the Journal were not infrequent:

"April 21. At Weaver's Hall a young man suddenly was seized with violent trembling all over and in a few moments sank to the ground. But we ceased not calling upon God till He raised him up full of peace and joy."

Again on May 21 he enters in his Journal: "In the evening I was interrupted at Nicholas Street almost as soon as I had begun to speak by the cries of one who was pricked at heart and strongly groaned for pardon and peace . . . Another person dropped down, close to one who was a strong assertor of the contrary doctrine. While he stood astonished at the sight, a little boy near him was seized in the same manner. A young man who stood up behind fixed his eyes on him and sank down himself as one dead, but soon began to roar out and beat himself against the ground, so six men could scarcely hold him."

On June 22 he writes, "In the society one before me dropped down as dead, and presently a second and a third. Five others sank down in half an hour; most of whom were in violent agonies. In their trouble we called upon the Lord and He gave us an answer of peace."

About sixty such cases of prostration are noted in the Journal, most of them occurring in small rooms where the crowd was great. There were a few in the open air around Bristol. The ministers looked upon such demonstrations as the rankest fanaticism, and even Whitefield wrote Wesley expostulating against them.

Wesley viewed some of these as of supernatural origin, though not all were so classed. "I relate just what I saw. Some of the circumstances seem to go beyond the ordinary course of nature. But I do not pre-emptorily determine whether they were supernatural or not. Much less do I rest upon them either proof of other facts or of the doctrines which I preached."

Blasphemers cried for mercy; sinners were smitten to the earth in deep conviction; even passing travelers were so affected. A physician studied a case of a woman whom he had known for years, and as he saw perspiration break from her face and her body shake he decided this was no mere physical disorder, but that it was evidence of God's workings.

During these weeks small societies were growing up which were modeled upon the Fetter Lane Society in London. There were two in Bristol, one on Nicholas and the other on Baldwin Street. Wesley saw the necessity of having a place for the groups to worship, and so he laid the foundation on which all of Methodism's churches throughout the world were to arise.

Taking possession of a piece of ground near St. James' Church in Horsefair, Bristol, he held it in the name of eleven trustees. At the time he did not realize the depth of this act's meaning, but as the years went by it became evident that here was the seed from which the systematization of his work was to come.

"On Saturday, May 12," he writes, "the first stone was laid with voice of praise and thanksgiving. I had not at first the least apprehension of being personally engaged either in the expense of the work or in the direction of it, having appointed eleven feoffees (trustees)."

In this, however, he was mistaken for the trustees were unable to raise money, and he was forced to undertake it himself. He also received letters from friends

in London and from Whitefield in particular which
urged him to do away with the trustees and hold the
property in his own name. Whitefield's concern for
this move was the fact that if the trustees should become dissatisfied with John's preaching, they could turn
him out of the building.

Thus all the early buildings of Methodism were held
by Wesley personally. Later by his Deed of Declaration all interests in his chapels were transferred to the
incorporated Conferences.

Nor was the new building to remain idle long, for
just three weeks after laying the cornerstone, Wesley
entered in his Journal, "Not being permitted to meet
in Baldwin Street, we met in the shell of our new society
room. The Scripture which came in course to be explained was, 'Marvel not if the world hate you.' We
sang:

> Arm of the Lord, awake, awake!
> Thine own immortal strength put on.

And God, even our own God, gave us His blessings."

Thus in Wesley's own building was held the first
meeting of his society. This was a mighty step forward
in his final break with the Church of England. The
little building was to have an interesting future. In it
during John's lifetime eighteen conferences were to sit,
and from the old pulpit he expounded the Acts of the
Apostles, which he declared to be "the inalienable
charter" of the Church of God. For many years this
was Charles' pulpit. Whitefield complained that the
room was too richly ornamented.

"The society room at Bristol," replied Wesley, "you
say is adorned. How? Why, with a piece of green
cloth nailed to the desk, and two sconces, for eight

candles each in the middle. I know no more. Now, which of these can be spared? I know not; nor would I desire less adornment or more. But 'lodgings are made for me and my brother.' This is in plain English . . . a little room by the school where I speak to persons who come to me, and a garret in which a bed is placed."

Wesley returned to London in June, 1739, where he preached indoors and out as opportunity was granted. In the autumn the weather turned unusually cold for open-air preaching. Two gentlemen invited him to speak in the city one November Sunday in a building then unused. Thirty years before, this had been a foundry where an explosion wrecked the building. The government moved the cannon works elsewhere and since, the building had been in ruins. Finally it was leased and afterwards restored and almost rebuilt at a cost of $4,000.

The preaching room would seat fifteen hundred. There was also a small band room seating three hundred. One end of the chapel was fitted as a schoolroom and on the opposite end was the book room. The "Collection of Psalms and Hymns," published in 1741, was imprinted "Sold at the Foundry, Upper Moorfields." Above the band room were John's apartments where his mother was to spend her declining years.

"I preached at eight o'clock to five or six thousand," he says of the first Foundry service on Sunday, November 11, 1739, "on 'The Spirit of Bondage and the Spirit of Adoption,' and at five in the evening in the place which had been the king's foundry for cannon. O hasten Thou the time when nation shall not rise up against nation, neither shall learn war anymore."

John now had the makings of a new movement which should center around his personality. His break with the Church of England was as complete as it could be until his death. He was in possession of his particular doctrine, and with two buildings, one at Bristol and the other at London, he was ready to launch forth in aggressive evangelism.

That Foundry was to be the pivot and headquarters around which John's movement was to revolve for thirty-eight years. It was to be superseded by City Road Chapel only when it was insufficient to meet the needs of the organization which John's personality brought into being. Time and again it was crowded out, until in 1775 Wesley obtained property some two hundred yards distant from the Foundry, and on a stormy April day, 1777, he laid the cornerstone of the City Road Chapel.

This new chapel, which was opened on November 1, the following year, was the pride of John's heart. When a preacher compared a Hull chapel to it, John replied tartly, "If it be at all equal to the new chapel in London I will engage to eat it."

Wesley viewed his work seriously, believing that his life had been channelized in the broad current of the divine will. He took the future in his stride, meeting opposition by evangelism, overcoming obstacles by organization. When preachers wrote against him he answered in kind, always keeping his ear attuned to the voice of the people who came to hear him.

He had undertaken a task as broad as any man's since Paul lost his head to Nero's axman. If the world was to be his parish it would demand the blessings of heaven upon his work as well as the proper organization of his converts into a dynamic force. The expediency which gave birth to the organization was already upon him.

Chapter VII

THE MASTER BUILDER

The Fetter Lane Society had already given John the practical plan by which to centralize his growing work. He had touched thousands with the Gospel, and to Wesley these people looked for spiritual guidance. Accustomed to societies within the Church, it was but natural for this form of organization to be the general outline which his movement was to follow. The Fetter Lane Society was strongly Moravian with a tincture of Wesleyanism. The Moravians outnumbered John's immediate followers; so it was but natural that the preponderance of influence should show in that direction.

Moravianism had sired Wesley's spiritual development, but its form was not broad enough to channelize the force of his widening personality and the achievements following his ministry. Problems came up in the Fetter Lane Society which resulted in a small group of Wesley's followers withdrawing from its fellowship. This was a nucleus which was to form the center of John's new group.

Near the close of 1739, eight or ten people came to Wesley, then in London, with a request that he should meet with them for prayer and counsel. Agreeing to do so he set aside Thursday evening for this purpose.

"The first evening," he says, "about twelve persons came; the next week thirty or forty. When they were increased to about a hundred, I took down their names and places of abode intending as often as it was con-

venient to call upon them at their houses. Thus without
any previous plan began the Methodist Society in England — a company of people associating together to
help each other to work out their salvation."

Remembering the words of the "serious man" who
had long ago during Oxford days told him, "The Bible
knows nothing of solitary religion," it was easy for
John to form his societies for spiritual advancement.
Early in April of that same year he had held meetings
with his converts for counsel and guidance. In Bristol
he took the names of three women who "agreed to meet
together weekly," along with the names of four men
who planned to do the same.

"If this be not of God, let it come to naught," he
had said at the time. "If it be, who can hinder it?"

The Bristol group was but the seed from which the
London Society was to spring, of which Wesley says,
"This was the rise of the United Society, first in London,
and then in other places."

This was a most worthy occasion, and John as always
was anxious to found it in Scripture. He felt his work
was moving in the general direction of that of the
Apostles.

"In the earliest times," he says, "those whom God
had sent forth preached the Gospel to every creature
. . . As soon as they were convinced of the truth as
to forsake sin and seek Gospel salvation, they immediately joined them together, took an account of their
names, advised them to watch over each other and met
those catechumens . . . apart from the great congregation that they might instruct, rebuke, exhort and pray
with them. . ."

Feet solidly resting on Bible grounds, he went forward rapidly. "Thus arose without any previous design on either side, what was commonly called a society; a very innocent name, and very common in London for any number of people associating themselves together."

When the Foundry society had begun, the first to be directly controlled by Wesley, the Fetter Lane group was still in existence; but trouble arose on July 20, 1740, which caused seventy-two of the members to unite with Wesley's group.

He had bound them together in a united whole, but he found a further step to be necessary. The people were widely scattered throughout London, and as such it was impossible for him to keep an oversight of their personal life. This gave birth to a new working Wesleyan unit, of which he says, "At length while we were thinking of quite another thing we struck upon a method for which we have cause to bless God ever since."

He broke down his parent society into smaller working units known as "classes." When this plan was outlined it was purposed for a different end altogether.

There was still a debt on the Bristol Horsefair meeting house, so John called together the principal men and asked how it could be met. Said one of the men, "Let every member of the society give a penny a week." Said another, "But many of them are poor and cannot afford to do it."

Captain Foy, the first speaker, suggested, "Then put eleven of the poorest with me and if they can give anything, well; I will call on them weekly and if they can give nothing, I will give for them as well as for myself. And each of you call on eleven of your neigh-

borhood weekly, receive what they give and make up
what is wanting."

While the stewards were visiting their eleven's for
money purposes, they caught rumors of how the men
were living. These lax conditions were reported to John,
who like a flash saw the spiritual implications of his
group plan. He said, "This is the thing; the very thing
we have wanted so long."

Immediately he called together the leaders of these
financial classes, unfolded his scheme and told them to
inform him as to how the people were living in their
groups. In London the same plan was put into opera-
tion April 25, when he called his leaders together and
perfected his mobile working forces. "This was the
origin of our classes in London," he states, "for which
I can never sufficiently praise God, the unspeakable
usefulness of the institution having ever since been
more and more manifest."

It was in this talent for organization that Wesley's
superiority over Whitefield is to be found. Whitefield
was the popular pulpit orator, speaking to as many as
sixty to eighty thousand people at a time. But he knew
little or nothing about uniting these forces in workable
and controllable units, while John understood the force
of small bodies and knew how to harness his man
power. Whitefield's work was soon dissipated while
Wesley's remains, for the latter built upon the foundation of linking man to man for workable schemes.

There would have been little or no Methodism without such a capacity. It was at this time that John began
using the term "Methodists" in reference to his followers. "I preached at Moorfields to about ten thousand,
and at Kennington Commons to, I believe, near twenty

thousand," he enters in his Journal for Sunday, September 9. ". . . at both places I described the real difference between what is generally called Christianity and the true old Christianity, which under the new name of Methodism is now also everywhere spoken against."

John soon found it impractical for the class leaders to visit each member at his own home; so it was decided to hold a weekly meeting at some central place, which caused them "to bear one another's burdens . . . And as they had daily a more intimate acquaintance, so they had a more endeared affection for each other."

The next step was the institution of weekly meetings for the class leaders, who were untutored men for the most part, "having neither gifts nor graces for such divine employment." For this purpose a Tuesday-night meeting was arranged, concerning which Wesley remarked, "It may be hoped they will all be better than they are, both by experience and observation and by the advices given them by the minister every Tuesday night, and the prayers offered up for them."

A forward step in binding the societies together was taken on February 23, 1743, when Wesley issued his General Rules. The society was defined "as a company of men, having the form and seeking the power of godliness, united in order to pray together, to receive word of exhortation and watch over one another in love . . ." The members were to evidence their desire for salvation "by doing no harm, by avoiding evil of every kind, especially that which is most generally practiced." They were also to "avoid such diversions as cannot be used in the name of the Lord Jesus."

John realizing that spirituality is engendered by use of the means of grace wrote this into his rules, and urged his followers to be faithful in public worship, attend to the ministry of the Word, partake of the Lord's Supper, fast and pray as well as conduct family and private prayers. In well-erected segments Wesley hereby laid the broad platform upon which his followers were to be molded into a church.

Wesley began to pay quarterly visits to the classes in 1742, during which time also the use of tickets of membership were issued. Shortly a voluntary division of classes into bands came about. Another revival from the ancient time was that of the love feast or *agape*, to which service only members holding class tickets were admitted. A little plain cake and water was used as a token of spiritual friendship which was followed by a service of Christian testimony.

Another feature which marked Wesley's work was a monthly watch night service, which he usually began between eight and nine and which continued until shortly after midnight. This meeting was based upon the references in the New Testament to the entire nights of prayer in which the Early Church engaged. This in time became a quarterly meeting, at length to form the current New Year's Eve watch night service.

Gradually it became necessary for John and Charles to make provision for their followers to receive the sacrament of the Lord's Supper. Very shortly Wesley was forced to separate his societies from the Church of England in that not only the Wesleys themselves were excluded from the parishes, but their members or followers as well. This is especially true after 1740. It therefore was their ministerial duty to supply the Sacrament to their converts who were thus denied this sacred privilege.

In the autumn a French clergyman offered John the use of his church at Wapping, where he and his brother administered the Sacrament on five successive Sundays to their members, now numbering a thousand or more. Charles performed the same duty for the Kingswood colliers in their school building. Being a good churchman he declared that were there no other places available he would conduct the sacred rite in the open air.

Performing this duty without the bishop's authorization brought the anathemas of the Church upon John's and Charles's heads. They were called before the bishops at London to answer for their actions. Samuel went so far as to declare that he would "much rather have them picking straws within the walls than preaching in the area of Moorfields" — referring to the half-witted actions of those incarcerated in insane asylums.

He wrote to his mother urging her not to join with them, saying, "I earnestly beseech the Almighty to preserve you from joining a schism at the close of your life . . . As I told Jack, I am not afraid the Church should excommunicate him, discipline is at too low an ebb, but that he should excommunicate the Church . . . He only who ruleth the madness of the people can stop them from being formed a sect in a very little time."

This represents the views of the clergy of John's day, as well as of his brother. The Church might be lax morally, but there was still enough life left in her to arouse the bishops when a schism was impending. Forgetful of the Church's seeming wrath for her wayward son, John went on with his message of redemption heralded for high and low alike. The glorious blessings of God walked by his side in this battle against evil.

Possibly the climax of Wesley's ill treatment at the hands of established ministers came when he visited Epworth, the scene of his birth. Going to services in the morning he offered to assist the rector, Mr. Romley, who had been schoolmaster at Wroote, but his offer had been declined. The house was packed at the afternoon meeting, for it had been rumored that John would bring the message. Instead the rector read a florid message against enthusiasm, directed at the visiting cleric and his followers.

The people would not be disappointed, for as they came out of the church, John Taylor announced that Wesley, not being permitted to preach from the pulpit, would speak at six that evening in the churchyard. When time for the service arrived, John climbed on his father's tombstone and delivered his message to the largest crowd ever seen at Epworth.

The scene was unique and inspiring — a living son preaching on a dead father's grave because a parish priest would not allow him to officiate in a dead father's church. "I am well assured," says Wesley, "that I did far more good to my Lincolnshire parishioners by preaching three days on my father's tomb than I did by preaching three years in his pulpit." The folk pressed him to remain longer, and for eight evenings he climbed on the tomb and delivered his messages. During the days he preached in the surrounding villages as occasion was granted.

Nor were results of those graveyard messages lacking. On the final Saturday evening, Wesley's voice was drowned by the cries of those seeking salvation. The last meeting continued for three hours, so tender the touch of heaven and the ties of friendship.

"We scarce knew how to part . . . Near forty years did my father labor here; but he saw little fruit of all his labor. I took some pains among his people . . . but now the fruit appeared . . . but the seed sown long since now sprung up bringing forth repentance and remission of sins."

John's time was divided between Bristol, Wales and London. It was on July 18, 1742, while speaking at Bristol, word reached him that his mother was very ill. Arriving home he discovered the noble woman verging on death and entered in his Journal, "I found my mother on the borders of eternity; but she has no doubt or fear, nor any desire but, as soon as God shall call her, to depart and be with Christ."

The end came the following Friday. Just before her light went out she said, "Children, as soon as I am released, sing a psalm of praise to God." She was buried in the Bunhill Fields, and as John said, "I commit the body of my mother to the earth," a great wail went up. She was gone, but her influence lingers as a sweet smelling fragrance to bless the labors of her son.

John's growing movement faced him with numerous problems, the most serious, once the Episcopal hands were off him, that of dealing with his members who felt the urge to ascend the pulpit and declare the message of God. He had no authority to make ministers of them by the laying on of hands. Time alone was to solve this problem. At his Kingswood School, Master John Cennick, son of a Quaker, had spoken several times without authority in 1739. But John thought little of this, feeling that his position as teacher gave Cennick unusual rights which did not adhere to other laymen.

While John excused Cennick, he did not think this had established a precedent. It was early in 1740, while his mother was still blessing his life with her earthly presence, word came to Bristol, where John was at the time, that Thomas Maxwell had presumed to preach before the Foundry Society. This alarmed John and so he rushed back to London where he sought to deal with the troublesome fellow.

Susannah met him, saying, "John, take heed what you do with reference to that young man for he is as surely called to preach as you are." Heeding his mother's words, Wesley attended a service where Maxwell was the speaker. He listened quietly to the message and then said:

"It is the Lord's doing; let him do what seemeth good. What am I that I should withstand God?"

Convinced that Maxwell was God's anointed minister, Wesley encouraged him by sanctioning his work as a lay preacher. This was the beginning of a remarkable rise of lay workers in Wesley's societies. Before the year was out there were twenty such preachers, heralding the doctrines they had learned from John. Among the outstanding ones was John Nelson, a stonecutter who had been converted under Wesley's ministry.

Once converted Nelson said, "If it be my Master's will, I am ready to go to hell and preach to the devils." It enraged the clergymen of the Established Churches to see a stonecutter preaching the Gospel, and doing it far better than they with all their boasted training. During one of Nelson's sermons he was set upon by bullies and almost beaten to death. Such were the persecutions which Wesley's lay workers faced to preach the Gospel.

As time passed John faced another problem, that of women preachers. True he had the example of Susannah who held forth in the Epworth pulpit — and did it more successfully than her Samuel. Mary Bosanquet, who married Fletcher of Mandeley, had opened an orphanage with her own money. She was assisted by Sarah Crosby, who with Mary began addressing members of the society. She asked Wesley's judgment on the matter, saying, "If I did not believe I had an extraordinary call, I would not act in an extraordinary manner."

This was in 1771 and Wesley replied that since she possessed "an extraordinary call" she should be free to continue her preaching. It was this divine *afflatus* which he recognized as the qualifying attribute for lay preachers.

While Wesley was building his movement on the line of establishing societies, Whitefield was in America traveling through the colonies with the evangelistic messages. He had much to do in bringing about the Great Awakening of the 1740's. Finishing his labors, George decided to return to England, which he did in March, 1741. He had a dogmatic bone to pick with Wesley, his fellow Holy Club brother.

Bone picking with John had become an old story, but for his adversary to arise from among his friends was a shock to the great Methodist. Whitefield returned from his contact with American Calvinism a militant advocate of the doctrine.

In answer John published his sermon on "Free Grace." The debate went back and forth with neither willing to lay down dogmatic arms until at length the two brothers parted as distant acquaintances. The result of the discussion is well summed up by Bishop

McTyeire, who says, "One branch" — Whitefield's — "after refreshing and enriching a dry and thirsty land, is absorbed and lost; the other" — Wesley's — "with well-defined and widening banks and deepening currents flows on."

Time, through the kindness of the Countess of Huntingdon, healed the breach, and George wrote to his friend, "May God remove all obstacles that now prevent our union; may all disputing cease, and each of us talk of nothing but Jesus and Him crucified . . . I find I love you as much as ever."

Years later the Countess, having already consulted Wesley about training preachers, established Trevecca College, of which John Fletcher was the president until the Calvinistic leanings of his benefactors caused him to retire.

Meanwhile Whitefield continued his evangelistic labors, and opened his Tabernacle, located in London, in 1756. Beneath the building were vaults, where Whitefield said "I intend to be buried, and Messrs. John and Charles Wesley shall also be buried there. We will all lie together. You will not let them enter your chapel while they are alive. They can do you no harm when they are dead."

When Whitefield died on September 30, 1770, at Newburyport, Massachusetts, Wesley complied with his wish and preached his funeral sermon in the Tabernacle. One day after Whitefield's funeral a lady approached Wesley and asked, "Do you expect to see dear Mr. Whitefield in heaven?"

To which John retorted immediately, "No, madam."

Somewhat taken back, the woman returned, "Ah, I was afraid you would say so."

"Do not misunderstand me," said Wesley, "George Whitefield was so bright a star in the firmament of God's glory, and will stand so near the throne, that one like me, who am less than the least, will never catch a glimpse of him."

The breach was healed, and even in this distant time there remains no scar. Both of the men in their sphere of service were supreme — one the mighty preacher, the other the wise executive.

CHAPTER VIII

FORWARD INTO A NOBLE FUTURE

It was but natural for the mobs to set upon Wesley and his workers — frowned upon by the clergy and opposed by the bishops. This was the price John was to pay for the victory of his success when England and the world took his movement to her bosom. Crowds came to hear his messages — five, ten and even twenty thousand — and with the crowds were the mobs. It is almost unbelievable the number of times John refers to the wrath of his enemies and the serious attempts even at his own life as well as that of his co-workers.

The Black Country in northern Staffordshire won notoriety as the early scenes of mob disturbances. Charles first preached at Wednesbury and John shortly followed. It was not long until a society of a hundred members was formed. Then broke the storm of persecution. Charles was preaching in Walsall when the crowd began shouting, roaring and throwing stones, many of which struck him.

This spirit followed elsewhere in the district, and wherever John or Charles appeared, the rioters turned out to smash windows, break furniture and rip through the houses. When John appealed to the magistrates for protection, he was informed it was the Methodists who brewed the riots and hence they must face the outrages alone.

A six-day riot broke out in that district while John was in London, of which he affirms, "I was not surprised at all; neither should I have wondered if, after the advices they had so often received from the pulpit as well as from the Episcopal chair, the zealous High Churchmen had risen and cut all that were Methodists to pieces."

Once while John was writing to a friend, the mob appeared before his house and clamored, "Bring out the minister; we will have the minister." John asked for someone to lead their captain to the room where he was. Soon the roaring lion became a meek little lamb. He then asked for others to be brought in and they too "were ready to swallow the ground with rage; but in two minutes they were as calm as he."

John then mounting a chair in the midst of the mob asked, "What do you want with me?" They answered, "Go with us to the justice." Returned John, "That I will with all my heart." When the crowd saw John's willingness to obey, some of the leaders said, "This man is an honest gentleman, and we will spill our blood in his defense."

When the group finally arrived at the magistrate's, he asked, "What have I to do with Mr. Wesley?" Finally someone blurted out, "To be plain, sir, if I must speak the truth, all the fault I find in him is that he preaches better than our parsons." Another offered, "He makes people rise at five in the morning to sing psalms. What advice would you give?"

"Go home and be quiet," was the answer.

Returning they were met by a mob from Walsall, who showed fight, and soon overpowered John's new friends. This left the preacher in the hands of his enemies once more. A big fellow struck at him several times with a heavy club, but missed. If the blow had taken effect Wesley says "it would have saved all further trouble. But every time the blow was turned aside, I know not how, for I could not move to the right hand or the left."

John was struck on the mouth, across the face, over the head, until blood gushed from open wounds, but he felt no pain. Dragged through the town, John made for an open door, which proved to be the mayor's, only to be denied entrance. This man thought his house would be torn down if Wesley entered.

When he gained the attention of the crowd, people began yelling, "Knock his brains out. Down with him. Kill him." Others shouted, "We will hear him once." When he began to speak he lost his voice suddenly, and the crowd was on him again. When strength returned John began to pray at the top of his lungs. A ruffian stepped to the fore and said, "Sir, I will spend my life for you. Follow me, and not one soul here shall touch a hair of your head."

When the ruffian and his friends escorted John to his lodgings in Wednesbury, he said, "I took no thought for one moment before another; only once it came into my mind that if they should throw me into the river it would spoil the papers that were in my pocket. For myself I did not doubt but I should swim across, having a thin coat and a light pair of boots. . .

"I never saw such a chain of providences, so many convincing proofs that the hand of God is on every person and thing, overruling all as it seemeth Him good."

Four brave Methodists decided to stand up and fight for John during these difficult times, resolved to live or die for him. When the mobs became the most riot-

ous, Wesley asked the men what they would do. William
Sitch gave answer: "To die for Him who died for us."

Such persecutions as these but cemented the Methodists into more closely knit units. Charles found them
after this disturbance "standing fast in one mind and
spirit, in nothing terrified by their adversaries. We
assembled before day to sing hymns to Christ as God
. . . It was a most glorious time."

George Clifton, captain of the rabble, who later rescued John, immediately forsook the godless crowd, and
when asked what he thought of John, said, "Think of
him? That he is a man of God; and God was on his
side, when so many of us could not kill one man."
Clifton lived to be eighty-five and to the end he never
wearied telling of that night when had not God stayed
his hand he would have taken Wesley's life.

John learned to eye these mobs. He had a rule
"always to look a mob in the face." When at St. Ives
a mob attempted to break up his meeting, he says, "I
went into the midst and brought the head of the mob to
the desk. I received but one blow on the side of the
head, after which we reasoned the case, till he grew
milder and milder and at length undertook to quiet his
companions."

At Plymouth-dock when the crowd became venemous,
John "walked down into the thick of them and took the
captain of the mob by the hand. He immediately said,
'Sir, I will see you safely home. Sir, no man shall touch
you. Gentlemen, stand off; give back. I will knock
down the first man that touches him'."

There seemed to be no limit to which this violence
went. Often they stoned Wesley; gangs set upon him
and, dragging him into alleys, would leave him for

dead. Once while preaching at Gwennap two men rode furiously into the congregation and laid hold of the people. As John commenced singing, one man cried, "Seize the preacher for His Majesty's service." When his servants were unwilling to do this, the leader jumped from his horse, seized John by the cassock and led him away three-quarters of a mile.

On finding John to be a gentleman, the man offered to take the preacher home, but Wesley declined this favor; so the man sent for horses and took John back to his preaching place. Wesley — undaunted by the bravado — arose to complete his service.

The sermons against John were as violent as the actions of the mobbers. At Bristol in 1743 a clergyman shuttled terrible messages at Wesley. Finishing his course the cleric was about to repeat them in the Church of St. Nicholas, when immediately on announcing his text, he was seized with a throat rattle, and falling backward in the pulpit, died the following Sunday. In other cases those who tried to wound or murder the preachers were themselves wounded or died at the hands of their companions in arms.

This violence continued until 1757 when peace reigned throughout the ranks of Methodism. This was brought about by the wise leadership and perfect command which John had over his forces. Isaac Taylor asserted, "When encountering the ruffianism of mobs and of magistrates, he showed a firmness as well as a guileless skill, which, if the martyr's praise might be of such an adjunct, was graced with the dignity and courtesy of a gentleman."

John's heroism was perfect, and not once was he forsaken by self-possession. The serenity of his temper, mobs could not ruffle. In the face of bravery and self-command the threatenings of the rabble could not stand. John always triumphed in the end. During those turbulent years when mobs fought him and clergymen condemned his work, Wesley went straight into the future, his mind racing with plans, his soul aflame with messages, the while busy binding his societies into a workable unit.

Wesley's idea of commanding the forces his soul energies had gathered about him was to be general of the movement. He kept in constant touch with his societies through sharp, officerlike letters to his preachers. Knowing the human heart, he read his workers and charted their abilities. Once he wrote to a preacher who had become controversial, saying, "Abstain from controversy; indeed you have not a talent for it. You have an honest heart but not a clear head."

It was only through this ability to bind preachers to him with the word of law that the gangling movement fused itself into the semblance of a living organism. Whitefield recognized this when he wrote, "My brother Wesley acted wisely. The souls that were awakened under his ministry he joined in societies, and thus preserved the fruit of his labor. This I neglected, and my people are a rope of sand."

He was able to achieve this unity of purpose only through a unity of command, and he was that commanding officer. His word became law to those who ministered under his flag. It was not, however, that he could not take censure, for this indeed he was able to do. Grace Murray, his last love, was in the habit of "telling me with all faithfulness and freedom if she thought anything amiss in my conduct."

Even the lash of Whitefield's tongue was bearable when he wrote, "Be humble; talk little; think and pray much." In retort John once said, "If anyone will convince me of my errors, I will thank him heartily." But until so convinced, his word must remain the intense fire which melted his movement into a service unit in God's kingdom.

Ofttimes he became so stringent and testy in his dictatorial assumptions that he was called in derision "Pope John." When necessary he could cut with the sting of a bullwhip, but in return, when others were as blunt and fiery as he, he did not resent it. Writing to Henry Venn, he affirmed, ". . . I sit down to answer your last . . . because it was wrote with so great openness. And herein you and I are just fit to converse together; because we both like to speak blunt and plain. . ."

From four A. M. until ten P. M. he allocated every moment of the day to religious duties, and hence he had little time for courtly speech or scintillant palaver. He must get straight to the issue and in doing so, often was accused of harshness.

This ability to compress long letters into telegram shortness rings with the clatter of a machine gun, as revealed in the following to Francis Wolfe, whom he had appointed second preacher of the Bristol circuit. Six weeks passed and the dilatory preacher made no appearance. Wesley wrote him, "Frankly, are you out of your wits? Why are you not at Bristol?" This produced the desired results.

Holding the reins over a growing group of lay preachers, which in the end numbered seven hundred, Wesley had to be forceful and dominant. To a flowery preacher who had strayed far afield from simple oratory, he wrote, "I hope you have now got quit of your queer, arch expressions in preaching, and that you speak as plain and dull as one of us."

His generalship extended even to advice to preachers on the masterly art of being profound yet simple. "Scream no more, at the peril of your soul," he advised a lay worker. "God now warns you by me, whom He has set over you. Speak as earnestly as you can but do not scream. Speak with all your heart; but with a moderate voice . . . I often speak loud, often vehemently, but I never scream. I never strain myself; I dare not; I know it would be a sin against God and my own soul."

Wesley laid the foundation of his success by absolute authority in command. Like a general, he asked for advice but always reserved the right to act upon it. Once during a quibbling session with a smaller soul who asked for a larger play of the democratic spirit, Wesley said, "If by absolute power, you mean power which I exercise without any coadjutor, it is certainly true, but I see no objection to it."

Following the marriage of Charles there was no one with whom he shared responsibility, for Charles was no longer free to travel as before. After the first difference with Charles when he disputed his right to marry, John made up his mind to suffer neither a superior nor any equal in authority over the movement. "From that time," says Whitefield, "he seemed determined to be *aut Caesar aut nullus*" — either Caesar or nothing.

In 1753 he wrote to his brother, saying, "I give you a dilemma. Take one side or the other. Either act really in connection with me, or never pretend it. . .

"By acting in connection with me, I mean, take counsel with me once or twice a year, as to the places where you labor. Hear my advice before you fix, whether you take it or not. At present you are so far from this that I do not know when or where you intend to go . . . And yet I may say without vanity that I am a better judge of this matter than either Lady Huntingdon, Sally Jones or any other. Nay, than your own heart. . ."

Charles slightly resented this and noted on the letter, "Brother, October 31st, 1753, trying to bring me under his yoke." John became even more dominant in his Conferences and once when Charles threatened to leave if laymen were allowed to take part in the discussions, John turned to his neighbor and remarked, "Give my brother his hat."

On the matter of Conferences Wesley recognized that his word must be final. Others might enter into discussions, but when John once spoke there was no appeal. While the breach between him and Charles was brief, there were others who disputed his right of rulership. During his own lifetime John determined to control the Conferences, but after his death he made disposition of rulership by affirming that Methodism was to be governed by the Annual Conference of preachers.

"You seem likewise to have quite a wrong idea of a Conference," he says writing to a dissatisfied preacher. "For above six years after my return to England there was no such thing. I then desired some of my preachers to meet me in order to advise, not control, me. And you may observe they had no power at all, but what I exercised through them.

"I chose to exercise the power which God had given me in this manner, both to avoid ostentation and gently to habituate the people to obey them should I be taken from their head. But as long as I remain with them, the fundamental rule of Methodism remains inviolate. As long as any preacher joins with me, he is to be directed by me in his work."

This guidance went even to the smallest matters, such as the selling of books. If John decided upon a course, or determined that the drinking of tea was a harmful practice for his people, then the contraband article disappeared from Methodist tables. In the matter of reading, he edited a Christian library, which he spoke of as a "complete library for those that fear God."

He decided that his preachers must be the promoters of book sales. And so wise was this executive order that John made vast sums of money from his writings and the sale of books. All of this, however, went back into the propagation of his work.

Writing to a preacher, he says, "You remember the rule of the Conference, that every assistant should take my books into his own hands, as having better opportunities of dispersing them than any private person can possibly have. I desire you would do this without delay."

Though John believed his authority over the societies to be full and complete, yet he delegated much of the pastoral oversight and control to class leaders, who relieved him of tedious problems and vexing details. His eye was keen in the discovery of preachers who could take executive and pastoral responsibility, and once glimpsed, they were pushed rapidly ahead of their brethren.

He did not greatly fear disruption, though at several times he was threatened with it. Once when trouble lifted its head, he said, "What if fifty of the preachers disjoined themselves? What should I lose thereby? Only a great deal of labor and care, which I do not seek, but endure because no one else either can or will."

Yet with all this dictatorial power Wesley had the universal esteem of his people. Southey expresses this sentiment in his biography, "No founder of a monastic order ever more entirely possessed the respect as well as the love and admiration of his disciples." He drew the converts to him with personal warmth flaming into affection.

It was one thing to unite individuals as such to him, but quite another to join the societies with something besides Whitefield's rope of sand. During the first five years of his itinerancy — 1739-1744 — Wesley had drawn forty-five preachers to himself, who supported themselves by working at their secular tasks in the intervals of their preaching journeys. In London alone there were two thousand members in the organization. Wesley's class meeting was in vogue, and the Rules for the societies had been published. The quarterly visitation of the groups had also been instituted. Places of worship had been secured and the Sacrament was administered.

In his forward look there was yet another step Wesley was to take, which came about in 1744 when he called the first Conference of his societies. John looked upon this London meeting as incidental, yet freighted with turbulent meaning. He entered in his Journal, "Monday, August 25, and the five following days, we spent in conference with many of our brethren, come from several parts, who desire nothing but to save their own souls and those that hear them."

That little Foundry conclave was the initiation of the famous Methodist Conference which have been the Church's executive backbone for almost two hundred years. There were present the two Wesleys, four other clergymen and four lay assistants. During this time they considered three things — what to teach, how to teach, and how to regulate doctrine, discipline and practice.

Doctrinal problems such as the fall, the work of Christ, justification, regeneration, and sanctification were fully discussed. Answering the "how to teach" problem, they decided that every sermon must invite, convince, offer Christ, build up the believer. This indeed was a large order for a single sermon, especially considering the fact that most of the ministers were untrained laymen.

The group wished to remain in the Church of England and one question was devoted to this. "Q. Do not you entail a schism on the Church? Is it not probable that your hearers after your death will be scattered into sects and parties? Or that they will form themselves into a distinct sect?"

The answer was formidable. "A. 1. We are persuaded the body of hearers will even after our death remain in the Church, unless they are thrust out. 2. We believe . . . either that they will be thrust out or that they will leaven the whole Church. 3. We do, and will do, all we can to prevent those consequences which are supposed likely to happen after our death. 4. But we cannot with good conscience neglect the present opportunity of saving souls while we live, for fear of consequences which may possibly or probably happen after we are dead."

Twelve rules were laid down for the guidance of lay assistants:

"1.   Be diligent; never be unemployed a moment; never be triflingly employed (never while away time); spend no more time at any place than is strictly necessary.

"2.   Be serious. Let your motto be: Holiness unto the Lord. Avoid all lightness as you would avoid hell-fire, and laughing as you would cursing and swearing.

"3.   Touch no woman; be as loving as you will, but hold your hands off 'em. Custom is nothing to us.

"4.   Believe evil of no one. If you see it done, well; else take heed how you credit it. . .

"5.   Speak evil of no one . . . Keep your thoughts within your own heart. . .

"6.   Tell everyone what you think is wrong in him. . .

"7.   Do nothing as a gentleman: you have no more to do with this character than with that of a dancing-master. You are the servant of all therefore.

"8.   Be ashamed of nothing but sin: not of fetching wood, or drawing water, if time permit; not of cleaning your own shoes or your neighbor's.

"9.   Take no money of anyone. If they give you food when you are hungry, or clothes when you need them, it is good. But not silver or gold. Let there be no pretence to say: We grow rich by the Gospel.

"10.   Contract no debt without my knowledge.

"11.   Be punctual: do everything exactly at the time. . .

"12.   Act in all things not according to your own will but as a son of the Gospel. As such, it is your part to employ your time in the manner which we direct: partly in visiting the flock . . . partly in such a course of reading, meditation and prayer as we advise from time to time. Above all, if you labor with us in our Lord's vineyard, it is needful you should do that part of the work we prescribe at those times which we judge most for His glory."

These rules were lengthy and detailed, but Wesley felt the lay workers were the heart of the Gospel appeal, and as such needed his guidance. It is interesting to note that they decided to spread the work by going "a little and little farther from London, Bristol, St. Ives, Newcastle or any other society. So a little leaven would spread with more effect . . . and help would always be at hand."

It was by this procedure that Wesley in his lifetime saw his societies cross England, reach into Ireland, Scotland and Wales and then leap across the ocean to America.

During this first Conference Lady Huntingdon invited Wesley and his group to her London mansion, which later under Whitefield was to be transformed almost into an aristocratic chapel. The second Conference went to Bristol, being held in the Horsefair preaching room. These two places, London and Bristol, had a monopoly on the Conferences until 1753 when Leeds shared the honor, and finally in 1765 Manchester vied with the other three cities. From then until Wesley's death all Conferences convened in one of these four places.

At the second Conference Charles's father-in-law, Marmaduke Gwynne, was present, and in 1749 the question was asked, "Who are the properest persons to be present at any Conference of this nature?" The answer listed three classes: as many preachers as possible, earnest and sensible band leaders of the Conference city and pious strangers who may be in the place.

In 1784 when Wesley drew up his famous Deed of Declaration the Conference was legally defined and a governing body of one hundred preachers was appointed. During many Conferences the question was debated as to leaving the Church of England. In 1746 Wesley renounced the doctrine of apostolic succession, which, in order to build upon lay ministers, became a strict necessity.

During the Leeds Conference in 1755 the problem of secession was discussed by the sixty-three preachers present, and in the end John's opinion prevailed that it was not expedient to withdraw from the Church. He did however express the prevailing sentiment: "Church or no Church, we must attend to the work of saving souls." For it was during the past year that some of the lay preachers had been administering the Sacrament.

The Church-leaving issue was merely shelved and by no means solved. At the Leeds Conference in 1769, memorable because of the appointment of the first preachers to America, John read a paper in which he advised the preachers what to do after his death. This was signed by the following three Conferences, and terminally was superseded by his Deed of Declaration. At this later date John expressed the opinion that sooner or later his followers would be forced to assume an independent relationship.

Many interesting sidelights develop from these Conference leadership sessions which reveal the nature of John's personality. At the 1766 Conference he faced the question: "What power is this which you exercise over both preachers and societies?"

"It was merely in obedience to the providence of God," he answered after tracing the majestic march of his work, ". . . that I first accepted this power which I never sought; it is on the same consideration, not for profit, honor, or pleasure, that I use it this day."

The matter of selecting proper lay preachers called for a definition as to abilities to be sought. "Q. How shall we try those who believe they are moved by the Holy Ghost and called of God to preach?"

"A. Inquire: 1. Do they know in whom they have believed? . . . Are they holy in all manner of conversation? 2. Have they the gifts as well as the grace for the work? Have they in some tolerable degree a clear, sound understanding? Have they the right judgment in the things of God? Have they a conception of salvation by faith? And has God given them any degree of utterance? Do they speak justly, readily, clearly? 3. Have they success? Do they not only so speak as generally either to convince or affect the hearts?"

At Leeds in 1766 Wesley was careful to impress upon his preachers the necessity of possessing a book-shelved mind, and entered in the minutes, "Read the most useful books . . . Steadily spend all the morning in this employ, or at least five hours in twenty-four . . . 'But I have no taste for reading.' Contact a taste for it by use or return to your trade." John was trying to make certain there were to be no preachers the feet of whose minds paced across their sermons with a leaden step.

It is noteworthy that all preachers in this group were mere assistants to Wesley. In an early Conference he determined that a preacher in charge of a circuit was called an assistant to himself, and his colleagues were helpers both to the assistant and to himself.

Wesley laid down the monetary rule when he said, "Take no money from anyone." While those early assistants did not vow themselves to perpetual poverty, they lived in such a state throughout their lives. They practiced a course of self-renunciation that outshines any of St. Francis' followers.

When a single preacher died in harness, leaving only one shilling and four pence, Wesley remarked, "Enough for any unmarried preacher of the Gospel to leave his executors." Married preachers, such as Nelson, the stonecutter, and Shent, a barber, worked at their trades for support. In 1752 the Conference fixed $60 (£12) a year as the amount the societies were to pay their preachers, which was raised in 1769 an additional $50 a year for the wife of a married preacher.

It is interesting that John was always on the lookout for little services he could perform for his preachers. This caused him to enforce a rule in 1774 that "every circuit shall find the preacher's wife a lodging, coal and candles, or £15 a year" to purchase these necessities, and later a $20-a-year allowance was given for each child.

The education of preachers' children called for consideration, and as a result of a $4,000 gift by a lady, the Kingswood school was enlarged with various facilities for the preachers' children in addition to those furnished the colliers' lads and lassies. This enlargement came about in 1748, when the most strict rules were enforced by Wesley for the control of students and teachers.

In this survey of preachers and their care we cannot pass without mention the fact that the 1763 Conference made provision for worn-out Gospel horsemen under the title of "superannuated preachers."

Wesley while caring for the forms of organization was anxious that the inner light be not dimmed in the hearts of his preachers. Early in his work (1747) he laid out a set of injunctions to guide the preachers' and stewards' daily work and Sunday activities. He felt that even with proper organization and executive control he could not afford to permit the preachers to lose the inner glow of their experience. These rules read as follows:

"1. You are to be men full of the Holy Ghost, and of wisdom, that you may do all things in a manner acceptable to God.

"2. You are weekly to transact the temporal affairs of the Society.

"3. You are to begin and end every meeting with earnest prayer.

"4. You are to do nothing without the consent of the minister (for guidance of stewards).

"5. You are to consider whenever you meet, 'God is here.'

"6. If you cannot relieve, do not grieve the poor."

When asked what would keep his work alive, John answered, "The Methodists must take heed of their doctrine, their experience, their practice, and their disciplines. If they attend to their doctrines only, they will make the people Antinomians; if to the experimental part of religion only, they will make them enthusiasts; if to the practical part only, they will make them Pharisees; and if they do not attend to their discipline, they will be like persons who bestow much pains in cultivating their gardens, and put no fence round it to save it from the wild boars of the forest."

He was not content that England alone should hear his story. Beyond England were other nations, edging the sea, and beyond the sea, America. These lands, too, John swept into the fold of his spiritual-life movement.

CHAPTER IX

CROWNED WITH VICTORY

It was natural that Wesley's spiritual progeny should carry his doctrines and societies wherever they went. Many of those early lay leaders or local preachers felt constrained to be heralds of John's movement in lands not yet touched by their sire's personal ministry. Before his death Wesley was to see practically all the islands which lie as gems around Britain brought into his workable fold. There was however one small group not so touched, and they were the Shetlands, north of Scotland.

Between Ireland and North England is the Isle of Man, on which a Liverpool local preacher, John Crook, preached the first Methodist sermon in 1775. It was two years before the busy John could chink in a visit to that section. His messages were greeted by massive crowds who came to hear him in churchyards, tumbled out into buying and selling marts and even jammed the fields that they might hear his words and, hearing, have spiritual life. So great was the imprint of John's foot on the Isle of Man that when he died, one-tenth of the populace were ranked as his followers.

The Scilly group, off the Cornwall coast, were blessed by a flying trip from John in 1743, when in company with Nelson, stonecutter turned parson, he preached to large groups and distributed little books and hymns. Here too were later to flourish societies which leavened the communities.

Immortal fame came from Wesley's work on the Isle of Wight where he formed his first society in 1753. Among the members was Robert Wallbridge, whose saintly Methodist daughter Elizabeth has been characterized in "The Dairyman's Daughter," which greatly influenced Queen Victoria, marked for God the early work of Moody and sent James Chalmers to a martyr's crown.

Nor were the tough-fibered Irish beyond the pale of John's influence. In Ireland he spent in all six busy years, having crossed the Irish Channel fifty times. Church bells rang when he first entered Dublin Bay on Sunday morning, August 9, 1747. In the afternoon he preached in St. Mary's Church "to as gay and senseless a congregation" as ever received his messages, and the next morning at six he spoke to a growing society of his own folk. Two weeks later he returned to Ireland only to find that a Catholic mob had wrecked the society's meeting room.

During the year Charles made some Irish headway, and when John returned the call in 1748 he found his work on a well-established basis and as he began preaching at five in the morning the people flocked to hear. Even at Philipstown, Clara and other places did the Catholic seek and find God, henceforth to march under the Wesleyan flag. It was not Catholicism he feared, "but the dead Protestantism of the land was a chief obstacle." John said, "O what a harvest might be in Ireland did not the poor Protestants hate Christianity (his militant brand) worse than either popery or heathenism."

His Irish visits during those early years were marked by mob violence. When he preached at Cork in 1750 the rabble rioted his services, and when he left for Bandon, the Corkites followed to hang him in effigy. The soldiers, many of whom were John's converts, became his greatest protection against the trouble-brewers. Within five years he had planted a firm society in Cork, built a large chapel, and John's followers were not only respected but feared in the city.

When he returned to Cork in 1787 so great was the change in attitude that he was received by the mayor and the chiefs of the city, "being no longer bitter enemies but cordial friends."

In 1752 he entered Dublin to be shocked at the "careless and indecent behavior of the congregation." Preaching at Kinsale, the soldiers carved with their swords a ledge of ground which served as a pulpit on the hill just back of the fort and the people packed the grassy slope.

Thus from city to city he besieged Ireland with the Gospel, at first to be mobbed, then feared and finally loved until shortly he was to be blessed with many well-watered societies. Preaching in Limerick, he spoke to the Palatines, German Protestant refugees who a generation earlier had been permitted to settle in the community. John's gospel took hold and opened new soul vistas to some.

Among the converts were Philip Embury, who became a local preacher, and Barbara Heck. When the colony migrated to America, Barbara took her religion with her, but it seems Philip lingered by the streams of the Nile with others who would forget in the new land their Old World doctrines. Barbara, one day, seeing Philip neglecting his local preacher's duties, felt concerned for his welfare and urged him to begin society meetings.

Hence from John's Ireland ministry was to sprout his first American contingent. It was thus always in propagating the Wesleyan movement.

Wesley was first invited to Scotland in 1751 at the instigation of Colonel Gallatin then at Musselburgh. Whitefield also urged John to make the journey affirming that he would "have nothing to do but dispute from morning to night," which, however, the preacher determined should have little place in his Scottish ministry. Wesley was a logician at heart and for him to thrust his mental sword at an opponent in debate, to see the other writhe in the agony of wordy defeat, brought him the greatest pleasure, next to the joy of winning a soul. This capacity was promoted by his position as Fellow at the University where he had charge of the debating classes.

When he began his Scottish ministry the congregations at Musselburgh "remained as statues from the beginning of the sermon to the end." At Edinburgh Wesley says he "used plainness of speech toward them and they all received it in love; so that the prejudice which the devil had been several years planting was torn up by the roots in one hour." When he returned to Glasgow two years later Dr. Gillis offered him his pulpit. Wesley's heart overflowed at this kindness.

"Surely with God nothing is impossible," Wesley said. "Who would have believed, five and twenty years ago, either that the minister would have desired it or that I should consent to preach in a Scotch kirk?"

On a future trip to Aberdeen, 1761, Wesley had the privilege of speaking at the college, where many were added to his society. The following morning he was accosted by a group of young ladies who told him that they had been unable to get into the previous meeting and requested him to speak to light their souls with the words of love.

"I knew not," says Wesley of the incident, "what God might have to do, and so began without delay on 'God was in Christ, reconciling the world unto himself.' I believed the words were not lost . . . In the evening the eagerness of the people made them ready to trample each other under feet. It was some time before they were still enough to hear, but then they devoured every word."

It was at Dundee in 1766 that he was forced to answer the numerous objections which had been thrust at him concerning Methodism in Scotland. His work had been so successful that many societies burst into bloom, as evidenced by a group of sixty members at Dundee.

"The sum of what I spoke was this," he says, writing later about his answer to the Scottish objectors. "I love plain dealing . . . I will use it now. I hang out no false colors; but show you all I am, all I intend, all I do. I am a member of the Church of England; but I love good men of every Church. My ground is the Bible. Yes, I am a Bible bigot. I follow it in all things. . .

"Therefore I always use a short private prayer when I attend the public service of God . . . Is this not according to the Bible? I stand whenever I sing the praise of God in public . . . I always kneel before the Lord my Maker when I pray in public. I generally use the Lord's Prayer, because Christ has taught me when I pray to say . . . I advise every preacher connected with me whether in England or Scotland herein to tread in my steps."

The following Sunday morning at Edinburgh he preached at five o'clock to the largest congregation he had ever spoken to before in the nation. Concerning this work he says, "It is scarce possible to speak too plain in England; but it is scarce possible to speak plain enough in Scotland. And if you do not, you lose all your labors."

It was this Scottish desire for controversy, especially as to their stand on doctrinal points, which slowed up the progress of Wesley's work in the nation.

He was also privileged as a spectator at several General Assemblies to see the Kirk of Scotland in action. Evidently the demeanor of the attending clergymen did not strike John as being in line with the occasion, for he says, "Had any preacher behaved so at our Conference he would have had no place among us."

In Wales John brought his initial message as early as 1739, and his first convert there was a poor woman who had walked six miles to hear him. At Cardiff he formed his mother church, but through Howell Harris and George Whitefield having pre-empted the Wales territory for their particular beliefs, Wesley's group has never been predominant in that section.

America was to be the great field of John's work, though personally he had little to do with its immediate development. In an extant 1769 letter he says, "There are only three Methodist societies in America: one at Philadelphia, one at New York and one twelve miles from it. There are five preachers there; two have been at New York for some time; three are lately gone over."

Appeals came from the new societies to Wesley that he send them Conference preachers. In the Leeds Conference of 1769 this is developed in form of question 13. "We have a pressing call from our brethren at New York (who have built a preaching house) to come over and help them. Who is willing to go?" Immediately two young men, one far gone with tuberculosis, volunteered for this over-seas service. To further this venture a collection was taken at the Conference.

When the volunteers Broadman and Pilmoor arrived in the new territory they set to work in dead earnest, following in the decisive steps of their spiritual father. When reports came to Wesley he was greatly pleased with them. During the coming months he faced the possibility of making the journey himself.

"It is not yet determined if I should go to America or not. I have been opportuned for some time . . . I must have a clear call before I am at liberty to leave Europe," he said. Tyerman writing of these American calls says, "Wesley had nearly arrived at the age of threescore years and ten; but if a way had opened he would have bounded across the Atlantic with as little anxiety as he was accustomed to trot to the hospitable Perronet home at Shoreham."

It was rumored John was seeking to make the American trip that he might assume the title of Bishop, which impingement of motive he cast aside with the brush of his mental hand. However, he faced a constant responsibility which he felt no one else could shoulder, and this was the fact that he alone carried the supervision of the English societies.

From time to time Wesley heard these American calls, but it was not until 1770 that the name of Francis

Asbury was read in the Conference. With Asbury's sailing for the New World, John's brightest light began a marvelous career of service which gave American Methodism its start.

When the struggle for independence came on, Wesley's relationship to the movement was not always the wisest. In fact his *Address to the American Colonies,* published by the many thousands, created a serious handicap for his American preachers.

"I am truly sorry," writes Asbury, "that the venerable man dipped into the politics of America. My desire is to live in love and peace with all men . . . However, it discovers Mr. Wesley's conscientious attachment to the government under which he lives. Had he been a subject of America, no doubt but he would have been as zealous an advocate of the American cause. But some inconsiderate persons have taken occasion to censure the Methodists in America on account of Mr. Wesley's political sentiments."

However it must be recognized that Wesley did plead the cause of the colonists, and had his letter of June 15, 1775, been given the same publicity as his *Address to Our American Colonies,* the feeling toward Wesley on this issue would have been far different than Asbury noted.

Writing to Lord North, Wesley said, "In spite of my long-rooted prejudices I cannot avoid thinking . . . that an oppressed people asked for nothing more than their legal rights, and that in the most modest and inoffensive manner that the nature of the thing would allow . . . I ask, Is it common sense to use force toward the Americans? . . . These men will not be frightened; and it seems they will not be conquered so easily as was at first imagined . . . and if they die, die sword in hand . . . They are as strong men as you . . . enthusiasts for liberty . . . The bulk of the people are so united that to speak a word in favor of the present English measures would almost endanger a man's life. . .

"These men think, one and all, be it right or wrong, that they are contending for their wives, children and liberty. . ."

Tragical indeed it was that this letter went unheeded by the English government, and was lost for a hundred years in governmental files. Had the colonies known Wesley's stand on this occasion, it would have made Asbury's work far easier than otherwise.

Wesley's American problem was seriously complicated after the Revolutionary War when the nation was rid of English bonds. There was a growing demand for a free American Methodism which could not long be stifled. The crisis came in 1784 when Asbury wrote Wesley, "We are greatly in need of help."

In response to this over-seas call, John made the wisest decision of his long career. In his study at City Road, Wesley first asked Dr. Thomas Coke, who for six years had been a Methodist preacher, to accept episcopal consecration and become superintendent of the American work. This innovation of ordination or consecration by Wesley so jarred the mental equilibrium of Coke that he asked for time to consider the proposal.

Wesley knew as well as Coke that the American societies needed someone with authority to ordain their ministers, and by this move would the need be supplied. Meanwhile Coke at Bristol gave the proposition due consideration and two months later mailed Wesley his answer of willingness.

Richard Whatcoat thus records the momentous step in his Journal: "September 1, 1784, Rev. John Wesley, Thomas Coke, and James Creighton, presbyters of the Church of England, formed a presbytery, and ordained Richard Whatcoat and Thomas Vasey deacons, and on September 2, by the same hands, etc., Richard Whatcoat and Thomas Vasey were ordained elders, and Thomas Coke, LL.D., was ordained superintendent for the Church of God under our care in North America."

The deed was done, and on arrival in America, Coke laid ordaining hands on Asbury, and they set up a joint superintendency or bishopric. Coke carried to America the following letter signed by Wesley:

"To all whom these Presents shall come:

"John Wesley, late Fellow of Lincoln College in Oxford, Presbyter of the Church of England, sendeth greeting. Whereas many of the People in the Southern Provinces of North America who desire to continue under my care, and still adhere to the Doctrines and Discipline of the Church of England, are greatly distrest for want of ministers to administer the Sacraments of Baptism and the Lord's Supper according to the usage of the said Church;

"And whereas there does not appear to be any other way of supplying them with ministers;

"Know all men that I, John Wesley, think myself to be providentially called at this time to set apart some persons for the work of the ministry in America. And therefore under the protection of Almighty God, and with an eye single to His glory, I have this day set apart, as a superintendent, by the imposition of my hands and prayer (being assisted by other ordained ministers), Thomas Coke, Doctor of Civil Law, a Presbyter of the Church of England, a man whom I judge to be well qualified for that great work. And I do hereby recommend him to all whom it may concern as a fit person to preside over the Flock of Christ.

"In testimony whereof I have hereunto set my hand and seal this second day of September in the year of our Lord one thousand and seven hundred and eighty-four. John Wesley."

This move greatly distressed Charles, and he wrote a quatrain:

> How easy now are Bishops made
> At man or woman's whim;
> Wesley his hands on Coke hath laid,
> But who laid hands on him?

In bitter mood Charles wrote Dr. Chandler about this strange move of his brother, saying, "After having continued friends for about seventy years and fellow-laborers for above fifty, can anything but death part us? I can scarcely yet believe it, that in his eighty-second year, my brother . . . should have assumed the episcopal character, ordained elders, consecrated a bishop, and sent him to ordain our lay preachers in America. . .

"Lord Mansfield told me last year that ordination was separation. This my brother does not and will not see; or that he has renounced the principles and practices of his whole life. Thus our partnership is dissolved, but not our friendship."

When John heard of the letter he immediately wrote his brother in defense of his actions, declaring that he was still an Episcopalian.

"I firmly believe I am a scriptural episkopos as much as any man in England or Europe . . . But this does in no wise interfere with my remaining in the Church of England; from which I have no more desire to separate than I had fifty years ago . . . I do indeed vary from them in some points of doctrine, and in some points of discipline; by preaching abroad, for instance, by praying extempore and by forming societies. . .

"I still walk by the same rule I have done for between forty and fifty years. I do nothing rashly. It is not likely I should. The high-day of my blood is over . . . Perhaps if you had kept close to me, I might have done better. However, with or without help I creep on" — sarcastically.

There was to be no real break between these noble brothers, both in their rank supremely gifted, for Charles attended the Conference of 1786, and was gratified when the ministers passed a resolution without a dissenting vote to remain in the Church of England.

"My brother and I," he wrote on that occasion, "and the preachers were unanimous for continuing in the old ship."

John was torn between his love for the Church of England with its forms, though he dissented from their dogma of apostolic succession, and his knowledge that the American church was demanding leadership who should be able to ordain ministers and assume other episcopal functions. His last words on the subject of the Established Church are these:

"I never had any design of separating from the Church; I have no such design now; I do not believe the Methodists in general design it . . . Nevertheless in spite of all I can do many will separate from it . . .

In flat opposition to them I declare once more that I live and die a member of the Church of England, and that none who regard my judgment will ever separate from it."

John had thus his final say on the subject, a say, however, which was disregarded by his societies across the Atlantic and upon his death was to be forgotten by his English followers.

Chapter X

TRAVELING THE GLORY ROAD

John Wesley was one of that large army of mighty, little men. When seventeen he was spoken of as "a very little fellow," and from then on he never grew any more. Never in his life did he stand over five-feet-five, nor weigh much over a hundred and twenty pounds. But into that small stature he packed the genius of an achieving man.

His was a long and glory-topped career. During the more than forty years he spent on horseback he traveled a quarter of a million miles. He preached forty-two thousand sermons and when the total of his books is summed they come to more than two hundred.

In John's prime he suffered a severe attack of tuber-culosis which caused him to compose the epitaph he thought would mar (grace) his tomb:

Here Lieth the Body
of
J O H N W E S L E Y
A Brand plucked from the Burning:
Who died of a Consumption in the Fifty-first Year
of his Age,
Not leaving, after his Debts are paid,
Ten pounds behind him:
Praying:
God be merciful to me, an Unprofitable Servant!
He ordered that this, if any, inscription should be placed
on his tombstone.

Thirty-four years later on his eighty-fifth birthday he thought back on the long trail which wound to the cradle that graced the Epworth rectory, recalling thirty-four years with practically no aches or pains, and he wrote in his Journal the sources to which he imputed his perfect health:

"1. To my constant exercise and change of air. 2. To my never having lost a night's sleep, sick or well, at land or at sea, since I was born. 3. To my having sleep at command, so that, whenever I feel myself almost worn out, I call it and it comes day or night. 4. To my having constantly for over sixty years risen at four in the morning. 5. To my constant preaching at five in the morning for above fifty years. 6. To my having had so little pain in my life, and so little sorrow or anxious care."

During the forty years of his horseback ministry, John rode on the average twenty miles a day, and often within the round of twenty-four hours he horsebacked as much as a hundred miles. He laid the secret of his tremendous accomplishments to the time-defying schedule with which he charted the course of his day. From his early injunction never to waste time he could not release himself. Checking through his Journal for instance on June 23, 1787, in his eighty-fourth year, we find this entry:

"Sat. 4:30, prayed, sermon. 8 tea, conversed, sermon; 2:30 dinner, conversed, sermon; 4:30 tea, conversed; 6 Matt. 13:33; 7 at Mr. Smythe's, sermon; 8 supper, conversed, prayer, on business; 9:45."

That was the log of a Wesleyan day and little did he deviate from such a schedule except to change the activities in which he engaged due to the exigencies of circumstances. To him time was all important, and once when he lost five minutes it required much water to run under the bridge of his life before he could forget those "five minutes lost forever."

He tutored himself to read while on horseback, and often as he jogged along the country roads of England his pen would be busy writing letters or even composing notes for sermons or articles that should in time find their way into books.

He knew England's highways and byways as no man of his generation. His innumerable hours hummed with the business of executing expeditiously the affairs of the societies. Thinking back through a hundred thousand miles of good horsemanship he discovered the secret of success with his mounts — "I rode with a slack rein." And in all this traveling he affirms that never had a horse stumbled with him, "except two, that would fall head over heels anyway." He goes on to say, "A slack rein will prevent stumbling, if anything will. But in some horses nothing can."

His *horse sense* (ability to read horses) evidently stood on as high an I. Q. level as his ability to read humans with whom the lot of his life was cast. A quaint picture indeed John made when as an old man he would jog along at an easy pace on a faithful mount, leaving the road to the horse's nose, while the rider's was deep in some book such as Priestly's *Treatise on Electricity*.

John loved horseflesh, even punctuating the spiritual admonitions of Conference minutes with practical advice about the care of animals, admonishing his preachers to save souls but to remember that every one "shall see with his own eyes his horse rubbed, fed and bedded."

How the man could find time to turn out of his mind's gristmill two hundred and thirty-three original works is more than one can understand, did not his Journal chart John's long career through those many ministerial years. Besides this the man had the habit of editing, paraphrasing, clipping and altering, and, as one biographer phrases it, "sometimes mutilating" the works of other men. Among these were 183 volumes which he sent through his thought machine, often hewing upon the mental output of others.

John's pen touched all subjects. He wrote many histories, English, Roman, etc., composed a book on logic, completed a text on primitive physic for the guidance of his people in matters of health. He wrote grammars of Hebrew, Greek, French and English along with an excellent English dictionary.

In January, 1778, he published the first volume of *The Arminian Magazine,* with the first editorial reading, "To the Reader. It is usual, I am informed, for the compilers of magazines, to employ outside covers in acquainting the courteous reader with the beauties and excellencies of what he will find within. I beg him to excuse me from this trouble . . . for writing a panegyric upon myself . . . I am content this magazine shall stand or fall by its own intrinsic value. . .

"It is usual likewise with magazine writers to speak of themselves in the plural number . . . And indeed it is the general custom of great men so to do. But I am a little one. Let me then be excused in this also and permitted to speak as I am accustomed to do. John Wesley."

Wherever John went his saddlebags were stuffed with cheap books which he sold or gave to the people. "Two and forty years ago," he says later in life, "having a desire to furnish poor people with cheaper, shorter and plainer books than any I have seen, I wrote many tracts, generally a penny apiece, and afterward several larger ones. Some of these have such a sale as I never thought of; and by this means I became unawares rich," all of which, however, he gave away.

In 1872 he and Coke started the first tract society, which is seventeen years before the Religious Tract Society of London was formed, and even forty years earlier, thousands of "Wesley's Word to a Smuggler," "Word to a Sabbath-breaker," "Word to a Swearer" and similar tract titles were in circulation.

During the years 1749-55 he edited a fifty-volume Christian Library, practically the only venture on which he lost money, the sum being a thousand dollars. Wesley's *Notes on the New Testament* is a classic for brevity and spiritual tone. This, along with his *Fifty-three Sermons*, forms the doctrinal standards of early Methodism. John was as much at home in the Greek Testament as in the English Bible.

His "Collected Works" in thirty-two volumes were serially published during the years 1771-74.

For forty years Wesley conducted a book store, which was first opened at the Book Room in the Foundry. When the City Road Chapel was erected the business was moved there in 1777. It was this which gave rise to the several Methodist publishing houses existing in various sections of the world.

Nor could John be idle in the field of sacred hymnology. When his own soul had tasted Pentecost in 1738, he and Charles issued a hymnbook for general use in their societies. This was to be followed by fifty-three other hymnal publications, which on the average is one each year until John's death. In 1778 the large hymnbook came out, titled "A Collection of Hymns for Use

of the People called Methodists." In this are 525 hymns
selected from twenty-one previous books which he and
Charles had written and edited.

Though John and Charles had many misunderstand-
ings, still these did not constitute a formal alienation
of each other's affections. To the end they were deeply
beloved of each other, which love is expressed by John's
"I have a brother who is as my own soul." They too must
be separated by death.

Charles called his wife to pen the words:

> Jesus, my only hope thou art,
> Strength to my failing heart:
> O could I catch a smile from thee,
> And drop into eternity.

Finishing the last note, the muse of song winged its
flight from his soul. A few days later he breathed,
"Lord — my heart—my God," lay back and fell asleep
in Jesus' arms on March 29, 1788.

Two weeks later John while leading a song service
gave out the words,

> My company before is gone,
> And I am left alone with Thee.

The eighty-five-year-old man's eyes flooded with tears
and, sitting down in the pulpit, he hid his face in his
hands. His brother, long beloved, was gone and John
was left alone.

Time did not dim Wesley's physical vigor, no less the
strength of his eyes. For instance, on May 9, 1777,
when in his seventy-fourth year he rode fifteen miles
from Osmotherly to Malton and preached a long and
tedious sermon. Hearing that a friend was ill, he started
immediately after the service to Otley, forty-eight miles
distant, which he reached at four A. M., having made
a sixty-three-mile journey in the course of twenty-four

hours. Nor was that long ride over, for the next day he returned to Matlon, rested an hour and rode to Scarborough, which he reached by evening. This day's jaunt was approximately a hundred miles.

Thus in forty-eight hours he had ridden a hundred and sixty miles or more.

Ten years later he outdid this for an endurance feat. From Sunday at midnight he traveled nineteen hours, and on Tuesday he was off again at four in the morning; on Wednesday he started once more at two, on Thursday at three and Friday at four A. M. During this time he was constantly traveling, covering in eighty hours two hundred and forty miles. To cap the week's journey he "went off with a gentleman to hear a famous musician that plays upon glasses."

It is but natural that a man who lived so long should at least have seasons when his heart was warmed in affection toward women. In John's life there was really but one woman who unlocked the memory-casket of his heart and she was the memorable Susannah, at whose funeral he spoke. However, he seemed to be possessed by a weakness for his nurses. There were three women who greatly moved Wesley's heart, and each of them was a nurse.

In Georgia there had been Sophia, who nursed him during a sick spell, and at once John's heart inclined toward her. In August, 1748, Grace Murray did him the honor of nursing him when he fell ill at Newcastle, and later Mrs. Vazeille cared for him while he was sick in London.

"I was taken ill at Newcastle," John writes of his proposal to Grace, "Grace Murray attended me continually. I observed her more narrowly than ever before

. . . I esteemed and loved her more and more. And when I was a little recovered I told her, sliding into it I know not how, 'If ever I marry, I think you will be the person.' After some time I spoke to her more directly. . ."

John shortly took Grace to the home of John Bennet, a lay preacher whom she had nursed two years before, saying that Bennet was to take good care of her. Such care Bennet did take of the nurse that Wesley never had the chance to marry the girl, for Bennet "jumped the matrimonial gun on him."

This fazed the love-life of John for some time, but on meeting Grace later she told him that she could not grasp the reality of his proposal, "nor could she possibly think what I proposed would ever come to pass."

And, of course, Charles had had his word to say about the proposed marriage of Brother John to Grace. Charles was thunderstruck at the thought of John's marrying "a servant, and one so low-born" — as Grace was. There were other good people who added their terrible mite to keep John from the snare of the woman's charms.

Having at length made up his mind to marry in 1751, he did so with the utmost dispatch. Again he suffered a sickness which called for the services of a nurse, said position being filled by Mrs. Vazeille. At the time John said, "I was clearly convinced I ought to marry," and four days later he said to Charles that he "was resolved to marry." And marry he did.

At once a storm arose over this step. John, however, could not be stopped by a mere tempest of words; so he went straight on in the deed. Married or no he saw no reason why he should change the course or tenor of his life. He entered in his Journal, "I cannot understand how a Methodist preacher can answer to it to God, to preach one sermon or travel one day less in the married than in the single state."

This was his policy and to it he remained true. He discovered things at home were not so smooth as they might be. The matrimonial boat rocked back and forth for several years until at length John's wife left him in 1771. Ten years later on October 12, 1881, this entry is found in the Journal: "I came to London and was informed that my wife died on Monday. This evening she was buried, though I was not informed of it till a day or two after."

Thus closes Wesley's connubial record, into which had been written many of the most disappointing hours of his life.

Wesley had been wedded in his early life to the only true love that should ever reign in his heart — the love of winning lost men to Christ. While others touched the springs of his emotions, the desire to win souls, to promote God's kingdom, to herald the true Gospel of salvation from sin, alone held his heart. He was a man who sought to keep the glow of God in his life shining at such white heat that others should recognize it and be led to seek the same transforming glory.

Here is the mark of him. Writing under date of January 22, 1789, he says, "God was eminently present with us at West Street Chapel." It was this presence of God for which he sought, and were a service not so marked, John's soul sensed it and he could not be content until the heavenly touch warmed the congregation. Later in the year he remarks concerning a crowded service where there were more people than the house would hold, "Truly God was there. . ."

It was this being constantly on tiptoe for the heavenly gleam that dominated Wesley's struggle to form his world parish. He sums up his doctrinal emphasis thus: "Our main doctrines, which include all the rest, are repentance, faith and holiness. The first of these we account as it were the porch of religion; the next, the door; the third, religion itself." It was this doctrine of Christian holiness, or Christian perfection, as Wesley termed it, which was the heart of his appeal. In his work, *A Plain Account of Christian Perfection*, he delineates his personal experience of holiness as well as outlines the development of the doctrine in his ministry.

Wesley's strength was to be found in the fact that he was *homo unius libri* — a man of one book, and that Book was the Bible.

"I am a creature of a day, passing, through life as an arrow through the air . . . I am a spirit from God, returning to God . . . God Himself condescended to teach me the way . . . He hath written it down in a Book. Oh, give me that Book! At any price give me the Book of God! I have it. Here is knowledge enough for me. Let me be *homo unius libri*. Here then I am far from the busy ways of men. I sit down alone. Only God is here. In His presence I open, I read His Book."

This catches the long cry of John's soul, that his outward life might be fully in accord with God, which spiritual alignment he refers to as Christian perfection.

Chapter XI

CLIMBING THE GOLDEN STAIRS

Wesley's house had been set in order. Around him he watched the Church, to which his spiritual genius had given birth, flourish as a seed plot for the dissemination of the true Gospel. Through the Deed of Declaration he had made provision for the continuity of Conference control by setting up a governing board of one hundred preachers.

Throughout England, Scotland, Wales and Ireland he had lifted his voice in fields, under the oaks, in dales, from hillsides, and had the joy of seeing his chapels dot the land from one end to the other. And now the end was just visible over the distant hills of eternity.

As a triumphant warrior he looked to it and was prepared. At the dawn of eighty he wrote, "I entered into my eightieth year, but blessed be God my time is not labor and sorrow. I find no more pain nor bodily infirmities than at five and twenty. This I still impute to (1) the power of God, fitting me for what He calls me to; (2) my still traveling four or five thousand miles a year; (3) to my sleeping night or day . . . (4) to my rising at a set hour; and (5) to my constant preaching, particularly in the morning.

"Lastly, evenness of temper. I feel and grieve, but by the grace of God I fret at nothing. But still 'the help that is done upon earth He doeth it Himself.' And this He doeth in answer to many prayers."

The next three years he was diligent in executing the affairs of the societies, superintending chapels and overseeing his workers. During this time he saw the American church flung into its noble beginnings. John also found time to carry the heavy load of preaching many times a week as previously.

When eighty-three in 1786 he makes a note that he is regretful for the decaying of his powers to such an extent that he cannot write more than fifteen hours a day without hurting his eyes. Two years later he refers to the fact that he is "not quite so agile as in times past." However, during the same year when friends urged him to take a carriage to his preaching appointment, six miles distant, from Bristol, he replied, "I am ashamed that any Methodist preacher in tolerable health should make a difficulty of this."

In his eighty-sixth year, during a nine weeks' tour of Ireland he preached a hundred sermons in sixty towns and villages as well as six times in the open air. Says a listener, "His spirit was as alert as ever, and he was little less the light of company he happened to be in than he had been twenty and three years before when I first knew him. Such unclouded sunshine . . . in the deepest winter of age and on the felt verge of eternity, bespoke a mind whose recollections were as unsullied as its present sensations were serene."

Among his other happy tasks was that of presiding during this journey over the Irish Conference (1789) of which occasion he wrote, "I found such a body of men as I hardly believed could have been found together in Ireland — men of sound experience, so deep piety and so strong understanding." Singing Charles's glorious hymn, "Come, Let Us Join Our Friends Above," he wrote the last word of his Irish ministry, and "they saw his face no more."

Following this he visited Cornwall churches. Where once they mobbed him, he had the privilege of seeing them stand in the streets as though a king were passing. Still as rugged as ever, during this year he preached to twenty-five thousand people at Gwennap pit. Here are some Journal entries during this year:

"June 22, 23, 24. I visited the classes now containing a little above a thousand members, after I had excluded about a hundred.

"July 10. We observed as a day of fasting and prayer chiefly for the increase of God's work. This was concluded with a solemn watch night wherein the hearts of many were greatly comforted."

On July 19 with the assistance of Dr. Coke he administered the Sacrament to eleven or twelve hundred communicants. There was thus no running out of his physical vigor nor his spiritual *elan*. His stamina steamed as full as though he were in his prime, as indeed he was in the heart of his spiritual manhood.

He entered 1790 with the step of victory and though he was then eighty-seven, on January 1 he wrote in his Journal, "I am now an old man, decayed from head to foot. My eyes are dim; my right hand shakes much; my mouth is hot and dry every morning; I have a lingering fever almost every day; my motion is weak and slow." He thus drones a song of weariness.

Reaching the major key of triumph he continues, "However blessed be God I do not slack my labor; I can preach and write still."

Nor did he change the routine of his life, for when four o'clock rolled around each morning John was up and at the tasks of the day after first seasoning his life with the usual morning prayer hour. That was to be a year of periods, when he closed sentences of his life, yet a year when the presence of God was dominant, which sense he expresses by a February 10 entry, "We found much of the presence of God. . ."

During February he sat for a last picture of which he says, "I submitted to importunity and once more sat for my picture. I could scarcely believe myself. The picture of one in his eighty-seventh year."

Then came a Scotland tour where he realized that he was drawing toward the sunset of his life. When his last birthday came, on June 28, 1790, he said, "This day I enter into my eighty-eighth year. For above eighty-six years I found none of the infirmities of old age, my eyes did not wax dim, neither was my natural strength abated." But during the past two years he said there had been a tumbling down of the tabernacle of clay, and thought his "natural strength would never return." Two days previous to this birthday he preached twice to large crowds.

As Wesley walked the golden stairs that led to eternity he was serene even to the end, doing with utmost care the tasks which he had faced for many decades. Conference duties called, and he conducted the last one at Bristol. Attaching his name to his final Conference record, he was off on a preaching mission which was to take him to Wales and finally to the Isle of Wight where he was delighted to meet "a poor, plain artless society."

Nor did his love for open-air preaching abate with age, for on October 7, 1790, he preached his last outdoor sermon under an ash tree at Winchelsea. Calling the service for noon so the workmen could attend, he took his text, "The kingdom of heaven is at hand; repent ye, and believe the gospel." Under that ash, known today as the Wesley tree, "the Word was with mighty power and the tears of the people flowed in torrents."

One who heard him preach during this last year of his life remarked that he formed a picture "of the kind, I never saw anything comparable to it in after-life." During the sermon his voice was calm, scarcely audible, and the people with reverence hung on his words as the venerable minister with his long white locks proclaimed the saving Truth.

John entered 1791 full of confidence even though his step was tottering and his constant prayer was, "Lord, let me not live to be useless." During January and February of this his last year he was busy as strength and occasion permitted, writing letters, preaching the Gospel and heralding redemption.

On January 3 he wrote a letter to Adam Clark, the Methodist commentator. On February 1 he posted his last American letter to Ezekiel Cooper, stationed at Annapolis, in which he said, "Those who desire to write or say anything to me have no time to lose, for time has shaken me by the hand and death is not far behind. But I have reason to be thankful for the time that is past. I have felt few infirmities of old age . . . And still am enabled to crawl a little, and to creep, though I cannot run. Probably I should not be able to do so much, did not many of you assist me by your prayers."

Still confident that time was on his side he arranged for a journey to Bath and a trip north which would cover many Sundays, though he was soon to start on another and an eternal journey. On Tuesday, February 22, he spoke his last sermon from the City Road Chapel pulpit, using the text, "Seek ye the Lord while he may be found; call ye upon him while he is near."

Thus John closed his ministry by calling seekers to find the Lord whom he had known as an intimate friend since May 24, 1738, when at Aldersgate God walked into his heart to be the consuming passion of his long life.

John to the end was an inveterate letter writer, for during his ministry he had penned thousands by which he directed the affairs of the societies, ruled his spiritual empire and bound hearts to him. His last letter was written to William Wilberforce, whose fight against slavery in the British Empire was at its height.

"Unless the divine Power has raised you up," he wrote, "to be an Athanasius, *contra mundum*, (against the world), I see not how you can go through your glorious enterprise in opposing that execrable villainy, which is the scandal of religion, of England and of human nature . . . O 'be not weary in well-doing.' Go on in the name of God and in the power of His might till even American slavery, the vilest that ever saw the sun, shall vanish away before it.

"Reading this morning a tract, written by a poor African, I was particularly struck by that circumstance — that a man who has a black skin, being wronged or outraged by a white man, can have no redress, it being a law in our colonies that the oath of a black against a white goes for nothing. . .

"That He who has guided you from your youth up may continue to strengthen you in this and all things, is the prayer of, dear sir, your affectionate servant, John Wesley."

Weakness overtook him on February 28 and he was taken to his City Road house where he became very feeble. One day he tried to write, but the pen would not go; so a friend suggested, "Let me write for you; tell me what you would say."

"Nothing," came the feeble reply, "but that God is with us." One by one friends came through the room, and, grasping their hands, John said, "Farewell, farewell." Several times he was heard to say, "I'll praise . . . I'll praise."

On Wednesday morning, March 2, as he neared the end, eleven persons gathered in the little room and John whispered, "Farewell," to be countered by Joseph Bradford's "Lift up your heads, O ye gates; and be ye lifted up, ye everlasting doors; and this heir of glory shall come in."

Without a groan, without a sigh Wesley had climbed the golden stairs that led to heaven's open door, and was in. The end of the long trail was the beginning of John's glad tramp through eternity's glory-decked domain.

As John lay in state in City Road Chapel, ten thousand people passed before his casket during the next week. Lest the crowd be too great it was decided to hold his funeral at five A. M. on March 9.

Dean Stanley tells how decades later he visited the City Road Chapel and asked the old caretaker to show him the cemetery where Wesley was buried. "I asked him," says the dean, "perhaps inadvertently and as an English Churchman might naturally ask —'By whom was this cemetery consecrated?' Said the sexton, "It was consecrated by the bones of that holy man, that holy servant of God, John Wesley."

There was nothing more to be said. John Wesley's bones not only consecrate that small spot of earth where they lie, but wherever his feet trod the militant path of righteousness he consecrated thereby the world.

For this purpose he climbed time's steep hills until his feet should stand by the redeemed hosts who ring heaven's corridors with peans of praise to Him whom John met at Aldersgate.

Printed in the United States of America